11.00

WITHDRAWN

KU-548-457

Term-time opening hours:

Tues, Thu 0845 - 2000

?

N 0014502 5

CHILD DEVELOPMENT
THROUGH PHYSICAL EDUCATION

By

JAMES H. HUMPHREY

Professor of Physical Education
University of Maryland
College Park, Maryland

NEWMAN COLLEGE
BARTLEY GREEN
BIRMINGHAM, 32.

CLASS	372.86
ACCESSION	75978
AUTHOR	HUM

CHARLES C THOMAS · PUBLISHER
Springfield · Illinois · U.S.A.

Published and Distributed Throughout the World by

CHARLES C THOMAS • PUBLISHER

BANNERSTONE HOUSE

301-327 East Lawrence Avenue, Springfield, Illinois, U.S.A.

This book is protected by copyright. No part of it
may be reproduced in any manner without written
permission from the publisher.

© *1980 by* CHARLES C THOMAS • PUBLISHER

ISBN 0-398-03981-X

Library of Congress Catalog Card Number: 79-20539

With THOMAS BOOKS *careful attention is given to all details of
manufacturing and design. It is the Publisher's desire to present
books that are satisfactory as to their physical qualities and artistic
possibilities and appropriate for their particular use.* THOMAS
BOOKS *will be true to those laws of quality that assure a good
name and good will.*

Printed in the United States of America

N-11

Library of Congress Cataloging in Publication Data

Humphrey, James Harry, 1911-
    Child development through physical education.

    Bibliography: p.
    Includes index.
    1. Physical education for children.   2. Child development.
I. Title.
GV443.H787   372.8'6   79-20539
ISBN 0-398-03981-X

PREFACE

I HAVE SPENT over four decades in the field of physical education, during which time my major thrust has been in the area of childhood physical education. It is the intent of this book to focus upon the place of physical education in the development of children—physically, socially, emotionally, and intellectually. To this end I have drawn heavily upon my own research and experience. In addition, I have resorted to the experiential endeavors of many others along with many scientific inquiries that have been reported in the literature.

From all of this I have derived what I consider to be the potential values of the great profession of physical education to child development. The reader should note that the key word is "potential" because it is my general feeling that we have done little more than "scratch the surface" of the latent possibilities of physical education in this regard.

A book is seldom the product of an author alone. Admittedly, the author does most of the things concerned with actually putting a book together, from the germ of the idea to eventually getting it published. However, it is almost always true that many individuals participate, at least indirectly, in some way before a book is finally "put to bed." This volume is no exception. To acknowledge everyone personally would be practically impossible. Therefore, I would like to acknowledge collectively the thousands of teachers and children who have in one way or another made this final volume possible.

A book of this nature should find use as a textbook in professional preparation courses and as a resource for physical education teachers, classroom teachers, and school administrators.

J.H.H.

CONTENTS

CHILD DEVELOPMENT
THROUGH PHYSICAL EDUCATION

Chapter One

AN OVERVIEW
OF PHYSICAL EDUCATION FOR CHILDREN

IT IS THE purpose of this book to examine the potential contribution of physical education to the developmental processes
of children in the age and grade ranges which comprise the
elementary school. These ranges are considered to be from
approximately age five to approximately age twelve and grade
levels from kindergarten to grade six. The following scale shows
the approximate ages of children at the various grade levels.

Grade	*Age*
Kindergarten	5 to 6 years
First Grade	6 to 7 years
Second Grade	7 to 8 years
Third Grade	8 to 9 years
Fourth Grade	9 to 10 years
Fifth Grade	10 to 11 years
Sixth Grade	11 to 12 years

It is important to be familiar with the ages of children at the
various grade levels, not only because of the relationship of age
and size, but children at the different levels tend to have certain
distinct characteristics. In consideration of the potential value of
physical education to development of children, it is imperative
that a general understanding of these characteristics be taken into
account.

GENERAL CHARACTERISTICS
OF ELEMENTARY SCHOOL CHILDREN

As elementary school children progress through various stages of development, certain distinguishing characteristics can be identified that suggest implications for physical education in the developmental process.

During the range of age levels from five through seven, children begin their formal education. In our culture a child leaves the home for a part of the day to take his or her place in school with children of approximately the same chronological age. Not only are these children taking an important step toward becoming increasingly more independent and self-reliant, but as they learn they move from being highly self-centered individuals to becoming more socialized members of the group.

This age is ordinarily characterized by a certain lack of motor coordination, because the small muscles of the hands and fingers are not as well developed as the large muscles of the arms and legs. Thus, as children start their formal education, they need to use large crayons or pencils as one means of expressing themselves. The urge to action is expressed through movement since the child lives in a movement world, so to speak. Children at these age levels thrive on vigorous activity. They develop as they climb, run, jump, hop, skip, or keep time to music. An important physical aspect at this level is that the eyeball is increasing in size, and the eye muscles are developing. This factor is an important determinant in the child's readiness to see and read small print, and, thus, it involves a sequence from large print on charts to primer type in preprimers and primers.

Even though children have a relatively short attention span, they are extremely curious about the environment. At this stage the teacher can capitalize upon the child's urge to learn by providing opportunities to gain information from first-hand experiences through the use of the senses. The child sees, hears, smells, feels, tastes, and *moves* in order to learn.

The age range from eight to ten is the period that usually marks the time spent in third and fourth grades. Children now have a wider range of interests and a longer attention span. While strongly individualistic, the child is working more from a position in a group. Organized games should afford opportunities for developing and practicing skills in good leadership and followership as well as body control, strength and endurance. Small muscles are developing, manipulative skills are increasing, and muscular coordination is improving. The eyes have developed to a point where many children can and do read more widely. The child is more capable of getting information from books and is beginning to learn more through vicarious experience. This is the stage in development when skills of communication (listening, speaking, reading, and writing) and the number system are needed to deal with situations both in and out of school.

During the ages of ten through twelve most children complete the fifth and sixth grades. This is a period of transition for most as they go from childhood into the preadolescent periods of their development. They may show concern over bodily changes and are sometimes self-conscious about appearance. At this range of age levels, children tend to differ widely in physical maturation and emotional stability. Greater deviations in development can be noticed within the sex groups than between them. Rate of physical growth can be rapid, sometimes showing itself in poor posture and restlessness. It is essential to recognize at this level that prestige among peers is likely to be more important than adult approval. During this period, the child is ready for a higher level of intellectual skills that involves reasoning, discerning fact from opinion, noting cause-and-effect relationships, drawing conclusions, and using various references to locate and compare validity of information. The child is beginning to show more proficiency in expression through oral and written communication.

Thus, during the years of kindergarten through completion of sixth grade, the child develops (1) socially, from a self-centered individual to a participating member of the group; (2) emotionally, from a state manifesting anger outbursts to a higher degree of self-control; (3) physically, from childhood to the brink of adolescence, and (4) intellectually, from learning by first-hand experiences to learning from technical and specialized resources.

If the child is to be educated as a growing organism, aspects of development need the utmost consideration in planning and guiding physical education learning experiences that will be most profitable for the child at a particular stage of development.

HISTORICAL BACKGROUND OF PHYSICAL EDUCATION FOR CHILDREN

In order to present a clearer picture of the place physical education for children occupies in the modern elementary school, it seems appropriate to discuss briefly its past development. Moreover, if we can see how the past has challenged the present, there is a strong likelihood that we may be able to understand more fully how the present might challenge the future.

There appears to be a widespread notion among some people at the present time that physical education for elementary school children is something new. This idea is probably prompted by the fact that physical education for children has been receiving more attention in recent years and by the further fact that more emphasis is being placed on it in some school systems.

Physical education for children at the elementary school level is not of recent origin. In fact, educators and philosophers as far back as the early Greeks felt that physical education activities might be a welcome adjunct to the total education of children. For instance, over 2,300 years ago Plato suggested that all early education should be a sort of play and develop around play situations.

In the seventeenth century, Locke, the English philosopher, felt that children should get plenty of exercise and learn to swim early in life. Rousseau, the notable French writer, held much the same opinion, believing that learning should develop from the activities of childhood. These individuals, along with numerous others, influenced to some extent the path that physical education for children was to follow through the years.

Throughout the ages, physical education programs have been caught between mere preparation of the body for combat and a recognition of the essential unity of mind and body in the educative process. In addition, there have been periods when any type of physical education program was abandoned purely on the basis that body pleasure of any sort must be subjugated, because this activity was associated with evil doing. The early American pioneers more or less typified this kind of puritanical thinking because there was no emphasis on physical education for the pioneer child in the way of formal education. Although physical education received no attention in the early American elementary schools, a series of factors over a period of years were instrumental in effecting a radical change, such as Western expansion, wars, application of inventions which revolutionized travel and communication, and the concentration of population, all having an influence on the growth of the early common schools. Although the early grade schools of the mid-nineteenth century were concerned predominantly with the purely academic subject matter of reading, writing, and arithmetic, the need for physical activity as a part of the school day was becoming evident. As a result, some time for physical exercises was allotted in the school programs of Boston as early as 1852. St. Louis and Cincinnati followed this procedure in 1855 and 1859, respectively. Interest on the state level began to appear, and a state law requiring physical education was passed in California in 1866. The fact that the general public was becoming conscious of the play needs of children was indicated by the establishment of the first public playground in Boston in 1885.

A short time later in 1889, in the same city, an interesting development occurred at a "Conference in the Interest of Physical Training." School administrators were beginning to feel the pressure and need for some kind of formal physical activity as a genuine part of the school program. Acting in a conservative manner at this conference, some school administrators proposed that a "physical training" program might be introduced as a part of the school day, but that it must consume only a short period of time, a minimal expenditure of money, and take place in the confines of the regular classroom. The Swedish pedagogical system of gymnastics, which was designed to systematically exercise the entire body in a single lesson, was proposed since this system satisfactorily met the criteria established by the school administrators.

On June 24, 1890, the Boston School Committee voted that this system of gymnastics be introduced in all of the public schools of Boston.   Although this proposal was a far cry from a well-balanced physical education program for children as we understand it today, it nevertheless served as a formal introduction of organized physical activity into the elementary school on the recommendation of school administrators.   It should be mentioned, however, that the main objective of physical education for children, in the eyes of the school administrators of that day, was that it should serve as a release from prolonged periods of mental fatigue.   It was believed that the main purpose of engaging in physical activity was to provide children with a "break" in the school day so that they would approach their studies with more enthusiasm and vigor.

In fact in 1895, Marion Holmes,[1] influenced by the previous fatigue studies of the German Burgerstein,[2] submitted research that indicated that the interjection of a short period of physical exercise served as a stimulant to the mental performance which followed.   This condition existed until such time that there was more widespread acceptance of the theory of mind-body relationship and the education of the *whole* person.   John Dewey, one of the early exponents of this principle, introduced the concept of a balanced physical education program for children while he was Director of the University of Chicago Laboratory School at the turn of the century.   Rather than only the more or less formalized gymnastics program, this school began to include games and dancing as a part of physical education for children.

However, up until the first world war, physical education programs for elementary school children, though few, consisted mainly of the formalized gymnastics and/or exercise types of programs.   The period between the two world wars saw more attempts at balancing physical education programs for children at the elementary school level with more emphasis being placed upon games and rhythmic activities.

After World War II a number of factors developed that were to bring the attention of the importance physical education had

---

[1]Marion Holmes, The fatigue of the school hour, *The Pedagogical Seminary,* vol. III, no. 2, October, 1895.

[2]Die Arbeits-Curve einer Schultstunde.   Vertrag von Dr. Leo Burgerstein.   Sonder-Abdruck aus "Zeitschrift für Schulgesundheitspflege," 1891.

for young children. One estimate indicated that from the period of 1945 to 1955 more published materials appeared relating to physical education for children than was the case in the preceding fifty years. In addition, many areas of the country began to provide for elementary school physical education workshops and other in-service education devices for elementary school personnel. In 1948, at its annual convention in Kansas City, the American Association for Health, Physical Education, and Recreation inaugurated an Elementary School Physical Education Section, and in 1951 the first National Conference in Physical Education for Children of Elementary School Age was held in Washington, D. C. (The term "Association" was recently changed to "Alliance" in this national organization.)

The period from 1950 to 1980 saw a continuation of the foundation that had been laid in the preceding years. Numerous national conferences, the appointment of an Elementary School Consultant by the American Alliance for Health, Physical Education, and Recreation, upgrading teacher preparation, and the recent "discovery" of the importance of *movement* in the lives of children have all contributed to better programs for children of elementary school age.

It should appear evident from this brief historical background that elementary school physical education has traveled a strange and sometimes hazardous road in reaching the level of importance that is attributed to it in modern education. However, in spite of various pitfalls, this area of education in the elementary school has forged ahead to the point where there has been almost unbelieveable and unparalleled progress in the past few years. This does not mean that the proponents for this area of education can become lethargic. Much needs to be done to continue to interpret the place and function of physical education in the modern elementary school curriculum, as well as to provide ways and means whereby physical education experiences can become even more valuable to the total development of the elementary school child.

CURRENT STATUS AND TRENDS

Current interest in physical education for children is perhaps at its greatest peak in history. It has been suggested that this interest is likely due to the following factors.

1. An increasing interest for the placement of physical education teachers in elementary schools.
2. The increasing number of clinics, institutes, and workshops involving motor experiences of children.
3. Large attendance at conferences, conventions, and meetings devoted to the topic of physical education for children.
4. Requests from elementary schools for assistance received by organizations at the national, state, and local levels.
5. The number of teacher education institutions seeking to provide more concentrated preparation in physical education for children of elementary school age.
6. An increased interest in preschool programs where motor activity is a very important aspect of child development.
7. The increased interest shown by disciplines outside the profession of physical education.

In summarizing this introductory chapter, it can be stated that as educators have become increasingly aware of the importance of a good physical education program for elementary school children, more emphasis has been placed on this area of the curriculum. As attention has been focused upon the potential value of physical education to the total development of children, a number of relatively new developments have emerged into certain trends:

1. With a better understanding of the importance of movement in the life of the young child, more emphasis is being placed upon these experiences at the preschool level.
2. Due to a greater awareness of some of the causes of learning disabilities, more attention is being directed to the perceptual-motor development of children.
3. Physical education is rapidly becoming a more important integral part of the experiences of the mentally retarded and the physically handicapped child.
4. Many important changes are being made in the area of

curriculum development in elementary school physical education.

5. More physical education teachers are keeping abreast with learning theory and making a greater attempt to apply these valid principles of learning to methods of teaching.

6. Teachers are recognizing more and more the value of the use of physical education as a learning medium in the development of skills and concepts in such areas as reading, mathematics, science, and social studies.

Chapter Two

A PHILOSOPHY
OF PHYSICAL EDUCATION FOR CHILDREN

W HETHER they know it or not, all individuals have developed some sort of philosophy of life. They may not have put it into so many words, but their philosophy is manifested in their daily actions. Regardless of the professional endeavor in which one chooses to engage, he or she will have some sort of philosophy about it. Thus, professional workers in the field of physical education maintain a philosophy about the field.

A standard dictionary definition of the term "philosophy" usually refers to it as *a pursuit of wisdom or enlightenment*. Another generalized description of the term is that it concerns our fundamental belief, or practicing those things in which we believe. More specifically, a philosophy of physical education is concerned with a careful systematic intellectual endeavor in which we attempt to see physical education as a whole and at the same time as an integral part of the culture of man.

My own philosophy (fundamental beliefs about physical education for children) is based upon many years of experience, along with a great deal of scientific inquiry into the various factors concerned with this area of childhood education. In my judgment, it is the duty of an author to provide for the reader a definitive discussion of his or her particular philosophy.

My philosophy of physical education for children has been depicted by what can be called, "A CONCEPTUAL SYSTEMS APPROACH TO ELEMENTARY SCHOOL PHYSICAL EDUCATION." This material was developed by Dr. James Schoedler of Wilmington, Delaware. He accomplished this by (1) listening to a series of thirty of my lectures, (2) participating in the demonstration of materials that I have developed, and (3) reviewing the literature and research contributed by me to physical education for children. As will be seen in the following discussion, Dr. Schoedler has utilized a series of *models* to assist in the visualization of my particular philosophy.

Models vary in reference from shapely females to mathematical formulas to three–dimensional structures of the human anatomy. In the materials presented here, models refer to two–dimensional graphic or schematic representations of a concept.

The main purpose of a model system is the management and control of information. The *forward feed* of information through a model is usually designated by two lower case letter *f*s. The *feedback* of information through the system is indicated by the single lower case *f*. The feedback path usually closes the loop of information, thus, it is termed the *closed loop path*.

A model represents a sequence, organization, or hierarchy of the *components* of a concept. The interrelationships of these components are depicted by their position to each other, either vertically, horizontally, or overlapping.

It is the intent of the model system, developed in the present material, to provide a total visualization of my concept of physical education for children and its related components. It should constantly be borne in mind that each interpreter will naturally apply models in different ways and to varying degrees based on his or her own individual concepts and experiences. This is to say that the autonomy of individuality in the application of a model system should be maintained. The creator of a model system has the responsibility for interpretation and explanation, whereas, the practitioner has the responsibility for individual interpretation and then application.

Model systems assist in interpreting the scope or parameters in making judgments regarding identity and clarification of the relationship of components. Model systems can also serve in (1) evaluating existing programs, (2) providing direction to correcting weaknesses, (3) teacher planning, (4) activity selection, and (5) curriculum development and other related endeavors, depending on the content of the model. The practitioner determines if the model system "works" and its true value through the application process.

In attempts to facilitate an understanding of physical education for children and its many complex components, physical educators have seldom turned to schematics as a representation of concepts. The material presented here was undertaken to provide a series of conceptual schematics of elementary school physical education and its components in order to bridge the gap between theory and practice and to serve as a tool to help solve problems in relating theoretical organizations to realities of physical education, first through the teacher who then communicates this to the child.

The model system developed here, which consists of eight models, includes an overview representing the total concept of elementary school physical education and individual models of its components. Each component of the total model, although autonomous with inherent goals and values of its own, is inter-related to other components as well as to the total model.

Model Number One

The first model (*see* Figure 1) is the overview of elementary school physical education depicting (1) the varying complexities children bring to physical education, (2) the components or branches of elementary school physical education, curricular, cognitive, and compensatory, and (3) the outputs observed in the form of affective, cognitive, and psychomotor behaviors all feed—back to the child, thus broadening the variations of children's backgrounds.

ELEMENTARY SCHOOL PHYSICAL EDUCATION: AN OVERVIEW

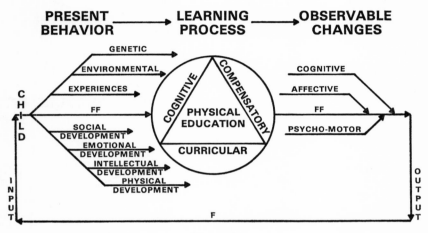

Figure 1.

Model Number Two

The second model (*see* Figure 2) represents the broad field of elementary school physical education and its three component branches. Curricular physical education is the basic branch; a valuable and worthwhile subject with the same status given to other areas of study in the elementary school. In the parenthesis under the heading is one standard classification of activities utilized in this branch. Cognitive physical education depicts the various academic areas that can be taught "through" the medium of physically oriented activities. Compensatory physical education can be referred to as education *of* the physical aspect of personality and designed for children with certain special needs such as perceptual-motor deficiencies. These three branches continue indefinitely, ever increasing in scope, program, and potential as depicted by the open-endedness of the cone.

ELEMENTARY SCHOOL PHYSICAL EDUCATION:
STRUCTURE OF KNOWLEDGE

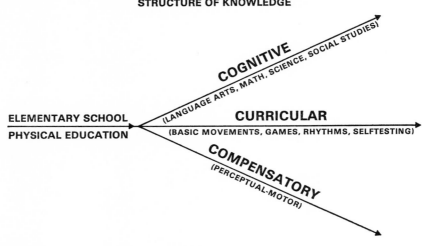

Figure 2.

Model Number Three

The major components of the child's total personality—physical, social, emotional, and intellectual—are shown in the third model (*see* Figure 3). The four aspects of personality are interrelated with the child's total development and elementary school physical education as shown by the overlapping circles. Each component, although a system in and of itself, is related to and influences a larger entity, namely, the total personality of the child and has implications for elementary school physical education.

CHILD GROWTH AND DEVELOPMENT THROUGH ELEMENTARY SCHOOL PHYSICAL EDUCATION

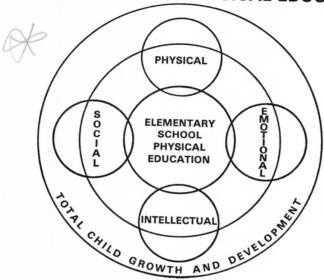

Figure 3.

Model Number Four

Children bring to the physical educator an infinite variety of combinations of characteristics, thus forming different behaviors and needs. Elementary school physical education must be both broad and flexible to accommodate these various populations of children. This phenomenon is represented in Model Number Four (*see* Figure 4) with the flow of individual characteristics contributing to the variance in populations that must be considered by the elementary school physical educator and program.

POPULATIONS SERVED BY ELEMENTARY SCHOOL PHYSICAL EDUCATION

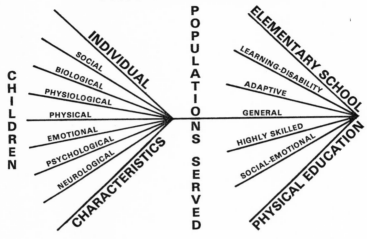

Figure 4.

Model Number Five

The learning process involves an observable change in behavior that is distinctly different after the learning experience as compared with the behavior prior to the learning experience. This process is shown in Model Number Five *(see* Figure 5) by the overlapping of these three phases along the forward flow from left to right. The observable change in behavior is feedback to effect the *present behavior,* which is shown as expanding with every learning experience by the outward growth of rectangles. The same continuous modification and changes in behavior following a learning experience is shown by the expanding rectangles.

THE LEARNING PROCESS

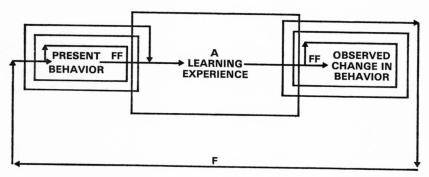

Figure 5.

Model Number Six

The teaching-learning situation with its implications for teachers is depicted in Model Number Six (*see* Figure 6). The phases of auditory and visual input include the children listening to and discussing verbal descriptions of an activity, and the prepared visual symbols and demonstration of skill or activity by either teacher or child. The opportunity for the children to participate in the activity, either individually or in a group, is the main part of the learning situation because it provides for direct purposeful learning. The evaluation phase includes a discussion of the activity with opportunities for leading questions and children's responses and interaction with the teacher and with each other. A teacher's evaluation of the learning situation can be valuable in the feedback process to affect future planning.

\CHING-LEARNING SITUTATION IN
ITARY SCHOOL PHYSICAL EDUCATION

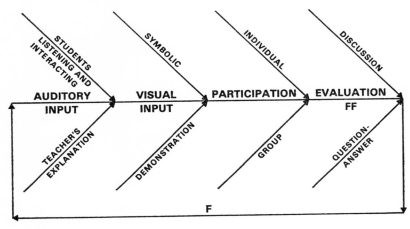

Figure 6.

Model Number Seven

The potential of using the medium of elementary school physical education in teaching academically oriented subjects is represented in Model Number Seven (*see* Figure 7). Elementary school physical education is shown piercing through the cone of learning and through the levels of learning, readiness, and academic learning. The open-ended cone represents the potential of relating and teaching "through" the physical education medium.

ACADEMIC LEARNING THROUGH ELEMENTARY SCHOOL PHYSICAL EDUCATION

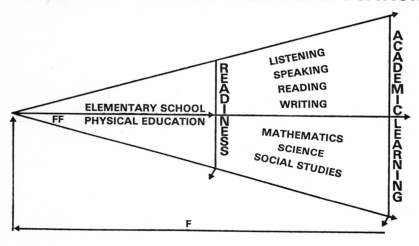

Figure 7.

Model Number Eight

The inherent facilitative factors of learning—motivation, proprioception, and reinforcement—and their implications for elementary school physical education are represented in the final model (*see* Figure 8). Children vary in the degree of development and refinement of the aspects of motivation, proprioception, and reinforcement (shown in parentheses), thus the open-ended cone to the left. The inherent facilitative factors are shown penetrating the spectrum of learning and influencing elementary school physical education.

FACTORS INFLUENCING ACADEMIC LEARNING THROUGH ELEMENTARY SCHOOL PHYSICAL EDUCATION ACTIVITIES

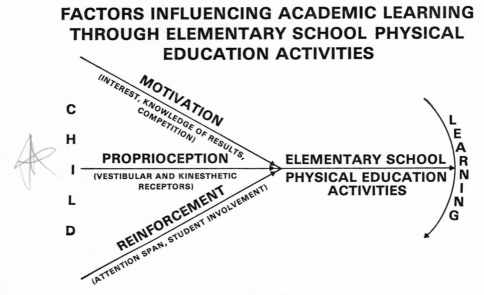

Figure 8.

In summary, it should be reiterated that each interpreter will apply the models in different ways and to varying degrees based on his or her own individual concepts and experiences. The autonomy of individuality in the application of the models should be maintained. The models presented here should be viewed in this general frame of reference. In subsequent discussions in the book these concepts will be dealt with in some detail. The reader may wish to refer back to the models from time to time for purposes of visualization of the concepts.

Chapter Three

A CONCEPT
OF TOTAL DEVELOPMENT OF CHILDREN
THROUGH PHYSICAL EDUCATION

IN ORDER to make a valid exploration of the area of physical education in the elementary school curriculum, it becomes necessary to consider the guiding philosophy and purpose of the elementary school as a whole. The necessity of this consideration lies in the fact that the basic philosophy that guides the entire educational program should also apply to physical education for children.

If one were to analyze the various statements of the purpose of elementary education, which have been made by responsible educational agencies and groups, it would be a relatively easy matter to identify a constantly emerging pattern. These statements through the years have gradually evolved into a more or less general agreement among present-day childhood educational leaders that the goal of elementary education is to stimulate and guide the development of an individual so that he or she will function in life activities involving vocation, citizenship, and enriched leisure; and, further, so that he or she will possess as high a level of physical, social, emotional, and intellectual well-being as his or her individual capacity will permit. More succinctly stated, the purpose of elementary education in our modern society should be in the direction of *total development* of the child during the formative years, which include kindergarten through grade six.

The ensuing sections of this chapter should be read with this general frame of reference in mind. This is to say that if it is a valid assumption that the purpose of elementary education is to attempt to insure total development of children, then it is incumbent upon us to explore the developmental processes as they relate to physical education. This chapter will overview generally these processes as they apply to physical education, while later chapters will go into detail on each of the developmental processes.

When it is considered that development of children brings about needs, and that these needs must be met satisfactorily, the importance of an understanding of development is readily discerned. When understanding the various aspects of development is accomplished, one is then in a better position to provide improved procedures for meeting the needs of each individual child. This implies that we might well be guided by what could be called a developmental philosophy if we are to meet with any degree of success in our dealings with children.

THE MEANING OF DEVELOPMENT

As mentioned previously, total development is the fundamental purpose of the education of children. All attempts at such education should take into account a combination of *physical, social, emotional,* and *intellectual* aspects of human behavior. In fact, the *Dictionary of Education* defines the term *child development as an interdisciplinary approach to the study of children, drawing upon such sciences as biology, physiology, embryology, pediatrics, sociology, psychiatry, anthropology, and psychology; emphasis is placed on the importance of understanding children through study of their mental, emotional, social, and physical growth; particular emphasis is laid on the appraisal of the impacts on the growing personality of home, school, and community.*[1]

Thus, the forms of development that I will consider in this text are the physical, social, emotional, and intellectual aspects. Of course, there are other forms of development, but perhaps they can be subclassified under one of the above areas. For example, *motor development,* which has been defined as a progressive change in motor performance, is considered as a part of the broader aspect of *physical development.* In addition, *moral development,* which is concerned with the capacity of the individual

---

[1]Carter Good, *Dictionary of Education,* 2nd ed., New York, McGraw, 1959, p. 167.

to distinguish between standards of right and wrong could be considered as a dimension of the broader aspect of *social develop-ment*. This is to say that moral development involving achievement in ability to determine right from wrong is influential in the individual's social behavior.

It seems appropriate at this point to comment on other terminology that is often used by physical educators to describe forms of development. Reference is made to what are ordinarily considered as the *learning domains*. These consist of the *affective* domain, the *cognitive* domain, and the *psychomotor* domain. Some writers refer to these as forms of development, i.e. affective development, cognitive development, and psychomotor development.

In this frame of reference, affective development is ordinarily thought of as being concerned with "appreciation" of movement and is sometimes referred to as a combination of social-emotional development. Cognitive development in this context means knowledge about movement or understanding why the body moves the way it does. Psychomotor development involves learning to move with control and efficiency, or more simply stated, skill in movement.

A great deal of clinical and experimental evidence indicates that a human being must be considered as a whole and not a collection of parts. For purposes here, I would prefer to use the term total personality in referring to the child as a unified individual or total being. Perhaps a more common term is *whole child*. The term total personality, however, is commonly used in the fields of mental health and psychology and recently has been gaining more use in the field of education. Moreover, when we consider it from a point of man existing as a person, it is interesting to note that "existence as a person" is one rather common definition of personality.

The total personality consists of the sum of all the physical, social, emotional, and intellectual aspects of any individual, i.e. the major forms of development previously identified. The total personality is "one thing" comprising these various major aspects. All of these components are highly interrelated and interdependent. All are of importance to the balance and health of the personality, because only in terms of their health can the personality as a whole maintain a completely healthful state. The condition of any one aspect affects another aspect to a degree and thus, the personality as a whole.

When a nervous child stutters or becomes nauseated, a mental state is "not" necessarily causing a physical symptom. On the contrary, a pressure imposed upon the organism causes a series of reactions, which include thought, verbalization, digestive processes, and muscular function. It is not that the mind causes the body to become upset; the total organism is upset by a situation and reflects its upset in several ways, including disturbance in thought, feeling, and bodily processes. The whole individual responds in interaction with the social and physical environment; and, as the individual is affected by the environment, he or she, in turn, has an effect upon it.

However, because of long tradition during which physical development *or* intellectual development, rather than physical *and* intellectual development, has been glorified, we oftentimes are still accustomed to dividing the two in our thinking. The result may be that we sometimes pull human beings apart with this kind of thinking.

Traditional attitudes that separate the mind and body tend to lead to unbalanced development of the child with respect to mind and body and/or social adjustment. What is more unfortunate is that we fail to utilize the strengths of one to serve the needs of the other. To better understand the concept of total personality in the human organism, a schematic diagram of the total personality may be seen in Figure 9.

The circle is the total environment of the individual that circumscribes and confines all aspects of the total personality. The triangle with its three sides—physical, emotional, and intellectual aspects of the total personality—form a single figure with the *physical* aspect as a base. An arrow extending from the center of the triangle upward through one of its sides is designated *social* to represent interpersonal relationships within the field of the individual and his environment. The arrow is pointed at both ends to suggest a two-way process: The individual is affected by those around him, and he affects them (largely through language as his

Figure 9.   Schematic diagram of total personality.

means of communication). The triangle is dependent upon a balance of all its parts, and if one part of the triangle is changed the entire triangle is reshaped. It is interesting to draw diagrams in which one after the other of the sides is shortened—as in one kind or another of developmental failure or retardation—and see how this affects the triangle. It is also interesting to make personal applications such as the following: "What happens to my intellectual performance when I am worried or have a stomachache? What changes occur in my body when I 'feel' frightened, embarrassed, or angered?" Obviously, similar applications can be made to children.

The foregoing statements have attempted to point out rather forcefully the idea that the identified components of the total personality comprise the unified individual. The fact that each of these aspects might well be considered as a separate entity should also be taken into account. As such, each aspect should warrant a separate discussion. This appears extremely important if one is to understand fully the place of each aspect as an integral part of the whole personality. The following discussions of the physical, social, emotional, and intellectual aspects of personality as they relate to physical education for children should be viewed in this general frame of reference.

THE PHYSICAL ASPECT OF PERSONALITY

One point of departure in discussing the physical aspect of personality could be to state that "everybody has a body." Some are short, some are tall, some are lean, and some are fat. Children come in different sizes, but all of them have a certain innate capacity that is influenced by the environment.

It might be said of the child that he "is" his body. It is something he can see. It is his base of operation—what was previously referred to as the "physical base." The other components of the total personality—social, emotional, and intellectual—are somewhat vague where the child is concerned. Although these are manifested in various ways, children do not always see them as they do the physical aspect. Consequently, it becomes ever more important that a child be helped early in life to gain control over the physical aspect, or what is known as *basic body control*. The ability to do this, of course, will vary from one child to another. It will likely depend upon the status of physical fitness of the child. The broad areas of physical fitness can be broken down into certain components, and it is important that individuals achieve to the best of their natural ability with these components. There is not complete agreement though of the identification of these components of physical fitness. However, the President's Council on Physical Fitness and Sports considers these components to consist of muscular strength, endurance, and power; circulatory-respiratory endurance; agility; speed; flexibility; balance; and coordination.[2] (These components will be discussed in detail in Chapter Seven.)

The components of physical fitness and thus, the physical aspect of personality can be measured by calibrated instruments,

[2]*Physical Fitness Research Digest,* President's Council on Physical Fitness and Sports, Washington, D.C., series 1, no. 1, July 1971.

such as measurements of muscular strength. Moreover, we can tell how tall a child is or how heavy he or she is at any stage of his or her development. In addition, other accurate data can be derived with assessments of blood pressure, blood counts, urinalysis, and the like.

THE SOCIAL ASPECTS OF PERSONALITY

Human beings are social beings. They work together for the benefit of society. They have fought together in time of national emergencies in order to preserve the kind of society they believe in and they play together. While all this may be true, the social aspect of personality is still quite vague and confusing, particularly where children are concerned.

It was a relatively easy matter to identify certain components of physical fitness such as strength, endurance, and the like. However, this does not necessarily hold true for components of social fitness. The components of physical fitness are the same for children as for adults. On the other hand, the components of social fitness for children may be different from the components of social fitness for adults. By some adult standards children might be considered as social misfits because certain behavior of children might not be socially acceptable to some adults. This is conversely true as well.

To the chagrin of some adults, parents, teachers, and others, young children are uninhibited in the social aspect of their personality development. In this regard, we need to be concerned with social maturity as it pertains to the growing and ever-changing child. This is to say that we need to give consideration to certain characteristics of social maturity and how well they are dealt with at the different stages of child development.

Perhaps we need to ask ourselves such questions as, "Are we helping children to become self-reliant by giving them independence at the proper time? Are we helping them to be outgoing and interested in others as well as themselves? Are we helping them to know how to satisfy their own needs in a socially desirable way? Are we helping them to develop a wholesome attitude toward themselves and others?"

THE EMOTIONAL ASPECT OF PERSONALITY

In introducing the subject of emotion, we are confronted with the fact that for many years it has been a difficult concept to define, and, in addition, there have been many changing ideas and theories in the study of emotion.

Obviously, it is not the purpose of a book of this nature to attempt to go into any great depth on a subject that has been one of the most intricate undertakings of psychology for many years. A few general statements relative to the nature of emotion do appear to be in order, however, if we are to understand more clearly this aspect of personality as it concerns physical education.

Emotion may be defined as *a response the body makes to a stimulus for which it is not prepared, or which suggests a possible source of gain or loss for him,* e.g. if a child is confronted with a situation and does not have a satisfactory response, the emotional pattern of fear may result. If one finds himself or herself in a position where desires are frustrated, the emotional pattern of anger may occur.

This line of thought suggests that emotions might be classified in two different ways: those that are pleasant and those that are unpleasant. For example, joy could be considered a pleasant emotional experience while fear would be an unpleasant one. It is interesting to note that a good proportion of the literature is devoted to emotions that are unpleasant. It has been found that in psychology textbooks much more space is given to such emotional patterns such as fear, hate, guilt, and anxiety than to such pleasant emotions as love, sympathy, and contentment.

Generally speaking, the pleasantness or unpleasantness of an emotion seems to be determined by its strength or intensity, by the nature of the situation arousing it, and by the way an individual perceives or interprets the situation. The emotions of young children tend to be more intense than those of adults. If an adult is not aware of this aspect of child behavior, he or she will not likely understand why a child may react rather violently to a situation that to an adult seems somewhat insignificant. The fact that different individuals will react differently to the same type of situation also should be taken into account, e.g. something that might anger one person might have a rather passive influence on another individual. In this regard, it is interesting to observe the effect that winning or losing has on certain children.

THE INTELLECTUAL ASPECT OF PERSONALITY

The word "intelligence" is derived from the Latin word *intellectus,* which literally means the "power of knowing." Intelligence has been defined in many ways. One general definition of it is *the capacity to learn or understand.*

Individuals possess varying degrees of intelligence, and most people fall within a range of what is called "normal" intelligence. In dealing with this aspect of the personality we should perhaps give attention to what might be considered as some components of intellectual fitness. However, this is a difficult thing to do. Because of the somewhat nebulous nature of intelligence, it is practically impossible to identify specific components of it. Thus, we need to view intellectual fitness in a somewhat different manner.

For purposes of this discussion, I would like to consider intellectual fitness from two different, but closely related points of view: first, from a standpoint of intellectual needs, and second, from a standpoint of how certain things influence intelligence. It might be said that if a child's intellectual needs are being met, then perhaps we could also say that he or she is intellectually fit. From the second point of view, if we know how certain things influence intelligence then we might understand better how to contribute to intellectual fitness by improving upon some of these factors.

There appears to be some rather general agreement with regard to the intellectual needs of children. Among others, these needs include (1) a need for challenging experiences at the child's level of ability, (2) a need for intellectually successful and satisfying experiences, (3) a need for the opportunity to solve problems, and (4) a need for the opportunity to participate in creative experiences instead of always having to conform. Some of the factors that tend to influence intelligence are (1) health and physical condition, (2) emotional disturbance, and (3) certain social and economic factors. When teachers have a realization of intellectual needs and factors influencing intelligence, perhaps then and only then can they deal satisfactorily with children in helping them in their intellectual pursuits.   It was mentioned that an important intellectual need for children is the opportunity to participate in creative experiences.   This need is singled out for special mention because the opportunities for creative experiences are perhaps more inherent in the physical education situation than in any other single aspect of the elementary school curriculum.

TOTAL DEVELOPMENT AND OBJECTIVES OF PHYSICAL EDUCATION FOR CHILDREN

The component elements of total development can satisfactorily emerge as valid physical education objectives for children. These elements have been expressed in terms of physical, social, emotional, and intellectual development comprising the total personality.   As such, they can logically become the physical, social, emotional, and intellectual objectives of physical education for children of elementary school age.

The term *objective* appears to have been adopted by education from the military.   The latter uses it to identify areas to be assaulted and/or captured in some way.   The *Dictionary of Education* gives the following definition of the term as *aim, end in view, or purpose of a course of action or a belief; that which is anticipated as desirable in the early phases of an activity and serves to select, regulate, and direct later aspects of the act so that the total process is designed and integrated.*[3] Various other terms are used to convey the same meaning.   Some of these include *aim, goal,* and *purpose.*   Regardless of the particular term used, we might well consider it with regard to a very simple meaning, e.g. what should we be trying to accomplish through the physical education medium where total development of children is concerned?

Although different writers have described physical education objectives in different ways and have placed greater emphasis upon some objectives than others, there seems to be certain basic points of agreement among all of them.   For example, most major

[3]C. Good, *Dictionary of Education,* 2nd ed., New York, McGraw, 1959, p. 371.

writers seem to agree on such points as the following:

1. Physical education should be a major educational force. It should be one of our country's most important means for educating children for what we as a people consider important in life.
2. A good program of physical education under well-qualified leadership should be available to all school-age children of both sexes.
3. Physical education is associated with the social, emotional, and intellectual aspects of the individual, as well as the physical aspect.

PHYSICAL OBJECTIVES

It may be stated generally that a good program of physical education can be considered as a stimulant to physical growth. Moreover, the general consensus indicates that participation in a well-balanced physical education program is one of the best known ways of maintaining optimum health.

It should be kept in mind that some children have great physical advantages simply because of the particular body build they may happen to have, and others may be at a relatively great disadvantage because of a very heavyset, or slight body build. Consequently, our objective should not be to make *every* child a great athlete. Rather, the physical objectives must be to help *each* child develop his or her individual potentialities for controlled and effective movement as fully as possible.

Two major objectives emerge out of the physical aspect of personality. The first of these takes into account *maintaining a a suitable level of physical fitness,* and, second, there is the consideration of the *development of skill and ability.*

Maintaining a Suitable Level of Physical Fitness

Physical fitness presupposes an adequate intake of good food and an adequate amount of rest and sleep; but beyond these things, activity involving all the big muscles of the body is essential. Just how high a level of physical fitness should be maintained from one stage of life to another is a difficult question to answer, because we must raise the question: "Fitness for what?"

Physical fitness has been perceived in different ways by different people, however, when all of these descriptions are put together it is likely that they will be characterized more by their similarities than by their differences. For purposes here, let us think of physical fitness as the level of ability of the human organism to perform certain physical tasks; or, put another way, the fitness to perform various specified tasks requiring muscular effort.

A reasonable question to raise at this point is: "Why is a reasonably high level of physical fitness desirable in modern times when there are so many effort-saving devices available that for many people strenuous activity is really not necessary anymore?" One possible answer to this is because all of us stand at the end of a long line of ancestors, all of whom at least lived long enough to have children. They were fit and vigorous and strong enough to survive in the face of savage beasts and savage men, in addition to hard work. Only the fit survived. Not very far back in your own family tree you would find people who had to be rugged and extremely active in order to live. Vigorous action and physical ruggedness are our biological heritage. Possibly, because of the kind of background that we have, our bodies simply function better when we are active.

Most child development specialists agree that vigorous play in childhood is essential for the satisfactory growth of the various organs and systems of the body. It has been said that "play is the business of childhood." To conduct this "business" successfully and happily, the child should be physically fit. Good nutrition, rest, and properly conducted physical education activity programs in school can do much to develop and maintain the physical fitness of children. Certainly, doing so is one of our major objectives.

Development of Skill and Ability

The second major physical objective of physical education has to do with disciplined bodily movement. The physically educated child, commensurate with his capacity and within his own limitations, is adept in a variety of physical education activities. Children enjoy those activities in which they are reasonably proficient. Thus, we are dealing with an important principle related to our physical education objectives: that is, if children are to enjoy participating in an activity, they need to be reasonably competent in the skills involved in the activity. Consequently, there must be objectives both in terms of the number of skills to which children at the different age levels are introduced and the level of competence to be achieved at that age level so that they may associate a pleasurable experience with participation.

We must reckon with another matter that is closely related to competence in a wide variety of skills. Some physical education teachers have stressed the very strenuous team sports in their programs and others have placed emphasis on what have been called "life-time sports" that may be used later on in life. A sensible point of view on this subject would appear to be that we should develop competence in a variety of skills for use "now and in the future." Stated more specifically, as an objective of physical education it could be said that all children should be prepared by their physical education experience to participate in suitable and satisfying activities for use now and in the future. Those individuals who would place undue emphasis on strenuous and violent activities at the expense of life-time activities for use in the future should pay special attention to the word "suitable" in the previous sentence. What is suitable during one period of life is not necessarily suitable during another. The intensely competitive, vigorous—and in some cases—violent sports are certainly not suitable during the elementary school years.

In summary, the physical objective of physical education should imply organic development commensurate with vigor, vitality, strength, balance, flexibility, and neuromuscular coordination, together with the development of skill and ability in a variety of physical education activities for use now and in the future.

SOCIAL OBJECTIVES

The school physical education "laboratory" (areas where activities take place) should present near ideal surroundings and environment for the social development of children. Why are people who are in the field of physical education convinced that this area of the school curriculum provides some of the very best means for teaching vital social skills? By their very nature, physical education activities are essentially socially oriented. If any type of physical education experience is to be successful and satisfying, the children involved must possess or acquire considerable skill in dealing with one another. They must learn to work together in the interest of the group. They must learn to accept and respect the rules of the games that they play. They must learn that sometimes it is necessary to place the welfare of the group ahead of their own personal desires. They must respect the rights of others. They must think and plan with the group and for the group. They must learn to win and lose gracefully.

In looking back over this list of social skills that is important in physical education activities, it should be discerned that it is just such social skills that are necessary for happy and successful social living everywhere. A qualified physical education teacher finds numerous opportunities to develop skills of interpersonal relationships that far exceed the basic essentials for successful play. Indeed, successful physical educators consider the development of increased social awareness and social skills as important objectives of their programs, and they make specific plans to reach these objectives. They recognize that physical education can have a profoundly humanizing effect upon children; participants quickly learn to evaluate their group members on the basis of what they can do and what kinds of persons they are rather than on the basis of their looks, race, religion, color, or economic status.

A brief summary of the social objective of physical education might imply satisfactory experiences on how to meet and get along with others, development of proper attitudes toward one's peers, and the development of a sense of social values.

EMOTIONAL OBJECTIVES

Most everyone recognizes that some physical education experiences can be highly emotionalized situations. For the child, there is the excitement that may be felt before certain kinds of physical education activities are initiated. When play is in progress, there is the thrill of making skillful moves and the possible disappointments or frustrations when one does not do well. Finally, the after-play emotions, determined to some extent by how well the child performed in relation to how well he or she thinks they can perform, but in almost all instances the pleasurable emotions caused by the good feeling that the time has been well spent.

From the point of view of physical education objectives, there are two very important things that might well be accomplished with the emotional aspect of personality. These may be classified as (1) to provide for fun and satisfying emotional release, and (2) to develop in children an increased capacity to control their emotions, thus contributing to the development of emotional maturity.

Fun and Emotional Release

Certainly one of the most important objectives of physical education should be wholesome fun. Moreover, it is a desirable objective of physical education to provide opportunities for children to enjoy uninhibited and vigorous movement. Because of their very nature, children require vigorous activity for proper growth and development. They should not be required to sit and listen for prolonged periods in the classroom without such activity.

Physical education should be primarily a learning experience for children, but its value as a means of easing emotional tensions in the form of genuine fun certainly should not be underestimated.

Emotional Control

It could be said that the major difference between a so-called "normal" individual and an incorrigible one is that the former has the ability to control his or her emotional impulses to a greater extent than the latter. Perhaps all of us at one time or another have experienced the same kinds of emotions that have led the abnormal individual to commit violence, but we have been able to hold our powerful and violent emotions in check. This may be an extreme example, but it should suggest something of the importance of emotional control in modern society.

It would appear that a reasonable and natural objective of physical education should be to help children increase their capacity to handle and control their emotions. The thoughtful physical educator is aware of educational opportunities offered in play situations for children to learn to deal with their own emotional arousals in socially acceptable ways. He or she helps to guide children in such a way that they learn to take pride in their ability to restrain themselves when necessary in order to abide by the rules of fair play and to behave like reasonable and decent human beings. The physical educator has real emotionally charged situations with which to work in order to teach children to deal with their strong emotions.

Another aspect of controlling the emotions is becoming able to function effectively and intelligently in an emotionally charged situation. Sometimes success in physical education experiences may hinge upon this ability, as does success in many other life situations. Extremes of emotional upset must be avoided if the child is to be able to think and act effectively. In physical education situations, children should learn that if they immediately put their minds to work on other things, such as group cooperation, they can then control their emotions.

In summarizing the emotional objective of physical education, it could be said that it should be implied that sympathetic guidance should be provided in meeting anxieties, joys, and sorrows, and help should be given in developing aspirations, affections, and security.

INTELLECTUAL OBJECTIVES

Of the contributions that physical education might make to the development of total personality, the one concerned with intellectual development has been subjected to a great deal of criticism by some individuals. Close scrutiny of the possibilities of intellectual development through physical education reveals, however, that a very desirable contribution can be made through this medium. This belief is substantiated in part by the affirmations made by many prominent philosophers and educators over a long period of years.

In a well-taught physical education lesson, there are numerous opportunities to exercise judgment and resort to reflective thinking in the solution of various kinds of problems. In addition, in a well-balanced physical education program, children must acquire a knowledge of certain rules and regulations in various kinds of games. It is also essential for effective participation that children gain an understanding of the various fundamentals and strategy involved in the performance of certain kinds of physical education activities.

Moreover, recent research has indicated that physical education activities provide a desirable medium for the development of concepts in subject areas such as reading, mathematics, science, social studies, and health and safety.

Indeed, physical education need not be considered an "all brawn and no brain" segment of the curriculum when it is realized that the various factors mentioned above have the potential to contribute substantially to the intellectual aspect of personality. In this particular regard, the following comment by the late eminent physiologist, Dr. Arthur Steinhaus, is worthy of note:

> "The sixty to seventy pounds of muscle that are attached to the skeleton of the average-sized man not only move him but also serve as his most important sense organ. Should this fact and all its implications become more fully understood and we shape our programs accordingly, physical educators will find their rightful place as one of the most distinguished contributors to the education of man."[4]

A brief summary of the intellectual objective of physical education implies the development of specific knowledge pertaining to rules, regulations, and strategies involved in a variety of worthwhile physical education learning experiences. In addition, this objective should be concerned with the value of physical education as a most worthwhile learning medium in the development of concepts and understandings in the other curriculum areas.

---

[4]A. Steinhaus, Your muscles see more than your eyes, *Journal of Health-Physical Education-Recreation,* September 1966.

Chapter Four

BRANCHES OF PHYSICAL EDUCATION
FOR CHILDREN

O VER THE years, physical education has suggested different things to different people. To some outside the field it may be thought of only as a series of "setting-up" exercises. To others it means only scoring touchdowns or hitting home runs. Even many educators are not entirely sure of its meaning, and oftentimes people in the field of physical education itself attach different meanings to it.

The time is long since past when physical education for children should be thought of only as a complete entity. For this reason, and for means of better communication, it seems necessary to identify certain branches of it. It should be understood that the branches of physical education for children suggested here are purely arbitrary. Some people may wish to add others or subclassify some of the branches suggested here, and, in the absence of anything resembling standardized terminology, it is their prerogative to do so. With this idea in mind, the branches used here are: (1) *curricular* physical education, (2) *compensatory* physical education, and (3) *cognitive* physical education.*

CURRICULAR PHYSICAL EDUCATION

This basic branch implies that physical education should be a subject in the curriculum in the same manner that mathematics is a subject or science is a subject, and so on. Such factors as sufficient facilities, adequate time allotment, and, above all, good

---

*I first introduced this classification of branches of physical education for children to the literature in the mid-1970s.

40

teaching should be provided so as to carry out the most desirable physical education learning experiences for children. A curriculum that is child oriented and scientifically developed should be provided as would be the case with the language arts curriculum or the social studies curriculum or any other curriculum in the school. It is in this branch that the child should learn to move efficiently and effectively and to learn the various kinds of locomotor skills, skills of propulsion and retrieval, and auxiliary skills needed for satisfactory performance in games, rhythms, and gymnastic activities.

Two natural subclassifications of the curricular branch could be "adapted" physical education and "extraclass" physical education. The term *adapted* means that special kinds of activities are adapted for use with children who have some sort of physical and/or mental impairment. The *extraclass* program, which would consist of the two broad categories of intramural activities (within the school) and interscholastic activities (between schools), should be a natural outgrowth of the regular physical education class program.

COMPENSATORY PHYSICAL EDUCATION

The term *compensatory* as it applies to education is not new, and over the years it has been used in a variety of ways. Possibly its derivation dates back to mid-nineteenth century Denmark.[1] At that time, what was known as the "compensatory education of cripples" involved the teaching of boys and young men with certain physical impairments such skills as basketmaking and shoemaking. The purpose was to prepare people who had certain deformities to be able to make a living on their own.

In this country at about the turn of the century it was reported that, "by compensatory education for deformed children is meant any special training which will make amends for their physical shortcomings and convert little cripples into men and women better fitted in some one direction to cope with fellow-man in the struggle for life."[2]

[1]*American Physical Education Review,* The education of crippled children, vol. III, no. 3, September 1898, p. 190-191.
[2]*American Physical Education Review,* The education of crippled children.

In recent years in this country, compensatory education has taken on a much different meaning, that is, it has been concerned essentially with "compensating" for an inadequate earlier education in some way or providing a better background for beginning school children who come from a low socioeconomic background. A case in point is the "Headstart" program sponsored by the federal government.

More recently, educators and psychologists in Great Britain have attached still a different meaning to compensatory education.[3] In this regard, Morris and Whiting have indicated that the term *compensatory education* now being used tends to replace the former term *re-education*. They contend that the term re-education was often misused when standing for compensatory education. Re-education implied educating again persons who had previously reached an educational level and who now for some reason did not exhibit behavior at a level of which they were previously capable. These authors assert that compensatory education implies an attempt to make good a deficiency in a person's earlier education and give as examples of this some of the structured perceptual-motor training programs that have originated in the United States.

It is from this source that I have derived the term *compensatory physical education*. The rationale for this term is that ordinarily the attempts to improve a deficiency in one's earlier education is likely to take place through the *physical* aspect of the individual's personality. Whereas the standard structured perceptual-motor training programs purport to improve learning ability through systematic exercises and procedures, compensatory physical education, as conceived here, seeks to improve upon learning ability through participation in regular physical education activities, although compensatory physical education should not be confused with what has been called "corrective" physical education or "adapted" physical education. The former has been used to correct certain physical impairments (flat feet, round shoulders, etc.) , while the latter means that the physical education program is adapted to meet the needs of those individuals who

[3]P. R. Morris, and H. T. A. Whiting, *Motor Impairment and Compensatory Education*. Philadelphia, Lea & Febiger, 1971, p. 9.

have certain physical and/or mental anomalies.

While compensatory physical education and cognitive physical education are based essentially on the same concept, the manner in which these two approaches are used should not be confused. It could be said that compensatory physical education is essentially concerned with education "of" the physical, while cognitive physical education is concerned with education "through" the physical.

Compensatory physical education attempts to correct various types of child learning disabilities which may stem from an impairment of the central nervous system and/or have their roots in certain social or emotional problems of children. This branch of physical education, most often through the medium of *perceptual-motor development,* involves the correction, or at least some degree of improvement, of certain motor deficiencies, especially those associated with fine coordination. What some specialists have identified as a "perceptual-motor deficit" syndrome is said to exist with certain neurologically handicapped children. An attempt may be made to correct or improve fine-motor control problems through a carefully developed sequence of motor competencies which follow a definite hierarchy of development. This may occur through the structured perceptual-motor program, which is likely to depend upon a series of systematic physical exercises, or it can occur through compensatory physical education, which attempts to provide for these corrections or improvement by having children engage in physical education activities where perceptual-motor developmental factors may be inherent. This procedure tends to be much more fun for children and at the same time is more likely to be free from emotionally traumatizing situations sometimes attendant in some structured perceptual-motor programs. In this regard, a comment by Dauer and Pangrazi is of interest.

> An effective physical education program will include in its normal format all of the movement elements inherent in perceptual-motor motor competency, and these elements are an important part of a very good physical education program and provide benefit for all children, particularly those in the lower grades. If children have these experiences within the physical education program there is little need

to structure a separate perceptual-motor program or to substitute such a program for normal physical education activities for children.[4]

The advantage of compensatory physical education is that it can be incorporated into the regular physical education program rather easily. It can be a part of the function of the physical education teacher, and, with assistance, the classroom teacher can handle many aspects of compensatory physical education.

The foregoing statements should not be interpreted as excessive criticism of structured perceptual-motor programs. Under certain conditions, and perhaps particularly in cases of severe neurological dysfunction, such programs can be useful. However, caution and restraint in the use of highly structured perceptual-motor training should be exercised, and these programs should be conducted under adequate supervision and by properly trained personnel.

Children Who Can Benefit from Compensatory Physical Education

We need to take into account the type of child who can receive the most satisfactory benefits from compensatory physical education. Ordinarily, those children who have certain problems in learning are placed in the broad category of slow learners. One classification of slow learners is (1) children with mental retardation, (2) children with depressed potential, and (3) children with learning disabilities. It is the third classification—children with learning disabilities—with which compensatory physical education is most vitally concerned.

Since classroom achievement of children with learning disabilities may be similar to those children who suffer from mental retardation and depressed potential, the problem of identification is of utmost importance. Johnson and Myklebust have warned of the imperative need for proper identification of these children by stating that, "Often the child with a learning disability is labeled slow or lazy when in reality he is neither. These labels have an adverse effect on future learning, on self-perception and on feel-

---

[4]V. P. Dauer, and R. P. Pangrazi, *Dynamic Physical Education for Elementary School Children,* 5th ed., Minneapolis, Burgess, 1975, p. 149.

ings of personal worth."[5]

The research identifying children with learning disabilities indicates that their achievement has been impaired in specific areas of both verbal and/or nonverbal learning, but their potential for learning is categorized as normal or above. Thus, these children with learning disabilities fall within the 90 and above IQ range in either the verbal or nonverbal areas. Total IQ is not used as the criterion for determining learning potential inasmuch as adequate intelligence (either verbal or nonverbal) may be obscured in cases where the total IQ falls below 90, but in which specific aspects of intelligence fall within the definition of adequate intelligence. The child whose IQ falls below the normal range and who has a learning disability is considered to have a multiple involvement.

A child with a learning disability has deficits in verbal and/or nonverbal learning. There may be impairment of expressive, receptive, or integrative functions. There is concern for deficits in the function of input and output, of sensory modalities and overloading, and of degree of impairment. The essential differences between the mentally retarded person and the child with a learning disability have been characterized as the following.

> One cannot deny that the neurology of learning has been disturbed in the mentally retarded, but the fundamental effect has been to reduce potential for learning in general. Though some retarded children have isolated *high* levels of function, the pattern is one of generalized inferiority; normal potential for learning is *not* assumed. In comparison, children with learning disabilities have isolated *low* levels of function. The pattern is one of generalized integrity of mental capacity; normal potential *is* assumed.[6]

Consequently, the child with a learning disability shows marked differences from the child with limited potential. There are both qualitative and quantitative differences. This child has more potential for learning, and the means by which he or she learns are different.

While there may be some overlapping in the educational

[5]D. J. Johnson, and H. R. Myklebust, *Learning Disabilities,* New York, Grune, 1967, p. 49.
[6]D. J. Johnson, and H. R., Myklebust, *Learning Disabilities,* New York, Grune, 1967, p. 55.

methods used with the groups identified as slow learners, there obviously must be differentiation in educational goals and approaches for these various groups. Correct identification of the factors causing slowness in learning is essential in teaching to the individual differences of children. The theories and practices labeled as compensatory physical education outline an effective approach for teachers working with the child appropriately identified as one with learning disabilities.

(Note: For a detailed account of compensatory physical education the reader is referred to: J. H. Humphrey, *Improving Learning Ability Through Compensatory Physical Education*, Springfield, Thomas, 1976.)

COGNITIVE PHYSICAL EDUCATION

This branch of physical education for children, which considers its use as a learning medium in other curricular areas, might well be considered a relatively recent innovation. In essence, this procedure involves the selection of a physical education activity in which a specific skill or concept of a given subject matter area has a relatively high degree of inherency. This physical education activity is taught to the children and used as a learning activity in developing the skill or concept in the specific subject area.

The Theory of Cognitive Physical Education

The important role of active play in cognition and learning has been recognized for centuries. In fact, the idea of the playing of games as a desirable learning medium has been traced to the ancient Egyptians. Throughout the ages, some of the most profound thinkers in history have expounded positively on the value of pleasurable physical activity as a way of learning. Perhaps one of the earliest pronouncements in this regard was Plato's suggestion that ". . . in teaching chlidren; train them by a kind of game and you will be able to see the natural bent of each."

The physical education learning medium is concerned with how children can develop skills and concepts in other school subject areas while actively engaged in certain kinds of physical education activities. Although all children differ in one or more characteristics, the fact remains that they are more alike than they are different. The one common likeness of children is that they all move. Cognitive physical education is based essentially on the theory that children will learn better when what we might call "academic learning" takes place through pleasurable physical activity. As mentioned previously, the procedure for learning through physical education involves the selection of a physical education activity, which is then taught to the children and used as a learning activity in the development of a skill or concept of a specific subject area. An attempt is made to arrange an active learning situation so that a fundamental intellectual skill or concept is being practiced in the course of participating in the physical education activity. Activities are selected on the basis of the degree of inherence of a skill or concept in a given school subject area, as well as the appropriate physical ability and social level of a given group of children.

Essentially, there are two general types of such activities. One type is useful for developing a specific concept where the learner "acts out," and thus is able to visualize as well as to get the "feel" of the concept. Concepts become a part of the child's physical reality as the child participates in the activity where the concept is inherent. An example of such an activity follows.

The concept to be developed is the science concept *electricity travels along a pathway and needs a complete circuit over which to travel.* A physical education activity in which this concept is inherent is *Straddle Ball Roll.*

The children stand one behind the other in relay files with from six to ten children in each file. All are in a stride position with feet far enough apart so that a ball can be rolled between the legs of the players. The first person in each file holds a rubber playground ball. At a signal, the person at the front of each file starts the activity by attempting to roll the ball between the legs of all the players on his team. The team which gets the ball to the last member of its file first, in the manner described, scores a point. The last player goes to the head of his file, and this procedure is continued with a point scored each time for the team that gets the ball back to the last player first. After every player has had an opportunity to roll the ball back, the team that has scored the most points is declared the winner.

In applying this activity to develop the concept, the first player at the head of each file becomes the electric switch that opens and shuts the circuit. The ball is the electric current. As the ball rolls between the children's legs it moves right through if all of the legs are properly lined up. When a leg is not in the proper stride, the path of the ball is impeded and the ball rolls out. The game has to be stopped until the ball is recovered and the correction made in the position of the leg. The circuit has to be repaired (the child's leg) before the flow of the electricity (the roll of the ball) can be resumed.

The second type of activity helps to develop skills by using these skills in highly interesting and stimulating situations. Repetitive drill for the development of skills related to specific concepts can be utilized. An example of this type of activity follows.

This activity is an adaptation of the game *Steal the Bacon* and can be used for practice on initial consonants. Children are put into two groups of seven each. The members of both groups are given the letters *b, c, d, h, m, n,* and *p* or any other initial consonants with which they may have been having difficulty. The groups face each other about ten feet apart as in the following diagram.

b		p
c		n
d		h
m	beanbag	m
h	(bacon)	d
n		c
p		b

The teacher calls out a word such as *ball,* and the two children having the letter *b* run out to grab the beanbag. If a player gets the beanbag back to his line, he scores two points for his group. If his opponent tags him before he gets back, the other group scores one point. The game ends when each letter has been called. The scores are totaled, and the game is repeated with the children being identified with different letters.

A very important precautionary measure with regard to cognitive physical education should be mentioned at this point, that is, this approach should be considered as only "one" aspect of physical education and not the major purpose of it. We should consider physical education as a subject in its own right, as is curricular physical education, which was discussed previously. Consequently, the use of physical education as a learning medium for other subject areas should not ordinarily occur during the regular time allotted to physical education. On the contrary, this approach should be considered a learning activity in the same way that other kinds of learning activities are used in a given subject area. This means that, for the most part, this procedure should be used during the time allotted to the particular subject area in question. Moreover, the classroom teacher would ordinarily do the teaching when this approach is used. The function of the physical education teacher would be to work closely with the classroom teacher and furnish him or her with suitable physical education activities to use in the development of concepts. This is to say that the classroom teacher is familiar with the skills and concepts to be developed, and similarly, the physical education teacher should know those activities as well that could be used to develop the skills and concepts.

Factors Influencing Learning
Through Cognitive Physical Education

During the early school years, and at ages six to eight particularly, it is possible that learning is limited frequently by a relatively short attention span rather than only by intellectual capabilities. Some children who do not appear to think or learn well in abstract terms can more readily grasp concepts when given an opportunity to use them in an applied manner. In view of the fact that children are creatures of movement and also that they are likely to deal better in concrete rather than abstract terms, it would seem to follow naturally that the physical education learning medium is well suited for them.

The above statement should not be interpreted to mean that I am suggesting that learning through movement-oriented experiences (motor learning) and passive learning experiences (verbal learning) are two different kinds of learning. The position is taken here that "learning is learning" even though in the physical education approach the motor component may be operating at a higher level than in most of the traditional types of learning activities.

The theory of learning accepted here is that learning takes place in terms of reorganization of the systems of perception into a functional and integrated whole because of the result of certain stimuli. This implies that problem solving is a most desirable way of human learning and that learning takes place through problem solving. In a physical education learning situation that is well-planned, a great deal of consideration should be given to the inherent possibilities for learning in terms of problem solving. In fact, in most physical education lessons, opportunities abound for near ideal teaching-learning situations because of the many problems to be solved.

Another important factor to consider with respect to the physical education learning medium is that a considerable part of the learnings of young children is motor in character, with the child devoting a good proportion of his attention to skills of a locomotor nature. Furthermore, learnings of a motor nature tend to usurp a large amount of the young child's time and energy and are often closely associated with other learnings. In addition, it is recognized by experienced teachers at the primary grade levels that the child's motor mechanism is active to the extent that it is almost an impossibility for him to remain for a very long period of time in a quiet state, regardless of the passiveness of the learning situation.

To demand prolonged sedentary states of children is actually, in a sense, in defiance of a basic physiological principle. This is concerned directly with the child's basic metabolism. The term *metabolism* is concerned with physical and chemical changes in the body that involves producing and consuming energy. The rate at which these physical and chemical processes are carried on when the individual is in a state of rest represents his *basal metabolism*. Thus, the basic metabolic rate is indicative of the speed at which body fuel is changed to energy, as well as how fast this energy is used.

Basal metabolic rate can be measured in terms of calories per meter of body surface, with a calorie representing a unit measure of heat energy in food. It has been found that, on the average, basal metabolism rises from birth to about two or three years of age, at which time it starts to decline until between the ages of twenty to twenty-four. Also, the rate is higher for boys than for girls. With the highest metabolic rate and, therefore, the greatest amount of energy occurring during the early school years, deep consideration should be given to learning activities through which this energy can be utilized. Moreover, it has been observed that there is an increased attention span of primary-age children during play. When a task such as a physical education experience is meaningful to a child, he or she can spend longer periods engaged in it than is likely to be the case in some of the more traditional types of learning activities.

The comments made thus far have alluded to some of the general aspects of the value of cognitive physical education. The ensuing discussions will focus more specifically upon what I call certain *inherent facilitative factors* in the physical education learning medium, which are highly compatible with child learning. These factors are (1) *motivation,* (2) *proprioception,* and (3) *reinforcement,* all of which are somewhat interdependent and interrelated.

Motivation

In consideration of motivation as an inherent facilitative factor of learning through the physical education medium, I would like to think of the term as an application of incentives to arouse interest for the purpose of causing a child to perform in a desired way.

I should also take into account "extrinsic and intrinsic motivation." *Extrinsic motivation* is defined as the application of incentives that are external to a given activity to make work palatable and to facilitate performance, while *intrinsic motivation* is the determination of behavior that is resident within an activity and that sustains it, as with autonomous acts and interests.[7]

---

[7]C. V. Good, *Dictionary of Education,* 2nd ed., New York, McGraw, 1958, p. 354.

Extrinsic motivation has been, and continues to be, used as a means of spurring individuals to achievement. This most often takes the form of various kinds of reward incentives. The main objection to this type of motivation is that it tends to focus the learner's attention upon the reward rather than the learning task and the total learning situation.

In general, the child is motivated when he or she discovers what seems to be a suitable reason for engaging in a certain activity. The most valid reason, of course, is that the child sees a purpose for the activity and derives enjoyment from it. Children must feel that what they are doing is important and purposeful. When this occurs, and the child gets the impression that he or she is being successful in a group situation, the motivation is intrinsic, since it comes about naturally as a result of the child's interest in the activity. It is the premise here that cognitive physical education contains this "built-in" ingredient so necessary to desirable and worthwhile learning.

The ensuing discussions of this section of the chapter will be concerned with three aspects of motivation that are considered to be inherent in physical education. These are (1) motivation in relation to *interest,* (2) motivation in relation to *knowledge of results,* and (3) motivation in relation to *competition.*

Motivation in Relation to Interest. It is important to have an understanding of the meaning of interest as well as an appreciation of how interests function as an adjunct to learning. The following description given some time ago by Lee and Lee expresses in a relatively simple manner what is meant by the terms *interest* and *interests:* "Interest is a state of being, a way of reacting to a certain situation. Interests are those fields or areas to which a child reacts with interest consistently over an extended period of time."[8]

A good condition for learning is a situation in which a child agrees with and acts upon the learnings that he or she considers of most value. This means that the child accepts as most valuable those things that are of greatest interest. To the very large majority of children their active play experiences are of the great-

[8]J. M. Lee, and D. M. Lee, *The Child and His Development,* New York, Appleton-Century-Crofts, 1958, p. 382.

est personal value to them.

Under most circumstances a very high interest level is concomitant with physical education situations simply because of the expectation of pleasure children tend to associate with such activities. The structure of a learning activity is directly related to the length of time the learning act can be tolerated by the learner without loss of interest. Physical education experiences by their very nature are more likely to be so structured rather than many of the traditional learning activities.

Motivation in Relation to Knowledge of Results. Knowledge of results is most commonly referred to as *feedback.* It was suggested many years ago that feedback is the process of providing the learner with information as to how accurate his reactions were.

Some years ago it was reported by Bilodeau and Bilodeau that knowledge of results is the strongest, most important variable controlling performance and learning, and, further, that studies have repeatedly shown that there is no improvement without it, progressive improvement with it, and deterioration after its withdrawal.[9] As a matter of fact, there appears to be a sufficient abundance of objective evidence that indicates that learning is usually more effective when one receives some immediate information on how he or she is progressing. It would appear rather obvious that such knowledge of results is an important adjunct to learning because one would have little idea of which of his or her responses were correct.

Cognitive physical education provides almost instantaneous knowledge of results because the child can actually *see* and *feel* himself throw a ball, or tag, or be tagged in a game. The child does not become the victim of a poorly constructed paper and pencil test, the results of which may have little or no meaning to him.

Motivation in Relation to Competition. Using games as an example to discuss the motivational factor of competition, I refer to my description of games, which is *active interaction of children in cooperative and/or competitive situations.* It is possible to have both cooperation and competition functioning at the same time, as

⁹E. A. Bilodeau, and I. Bilodeau, Motor skill learning, *Annual Review of Psychology,* Palo Alto, 1961, p. 243-270.

in the case of team games. While one team is competing against the other, there is cooperation within each group. In this framework it could be said that a child is learning to cooperate while competing. It is also possible to have one group competing against another without cooperation within the group, as in the case of games where all children run for a goal line independently and on their own.

The terms *cooperation* and *competition* are antonymous; therefore, the reconciliation of children's competitive needs and cooperative needs is not an easy matter. In a sense, we are confronted with an ambivalent condition, which, if not carefully handled, could place children in a state of conflict.

Modern society not only rewards one kind of behavior (cooperation), but also its direct opposite (competition). Perhaps more often than not our cultural demands sanction these rewards without provision for clear-cut standards with regard to specific conditions under which these forms of behavior might well be practiced. Hence, the child is placed in somewhat of a quandary with reference to when to cooperate and when to compete.

The competitive aspects of physical education not only appear to be a good medium for learning, because of the intrinsic motivation inherent in them, but also this medium of learning can provide for competitive needs of children in a pleasurable and enjoyable way.

Proprioception

Earlier in this chapter it was stated that the theory of learning accepted here takes place in terms of a reorganization of the systems of perception into a functional and integrated whole as a result of certain stimuli. These systems of perception, or sensory processes as they are sometimes referred to, are ordinarily considered to consist of the senses of sight, hearing, touch, smell, and taste. Although this point of view is convenient for some purposes, it greatly oversimplifies the ways by which information can be fed into the human organism; that is, there are a number of sources of sensory input that are overlooked, particularly the senses that enable the body to maintain its correct posture.[10] As a matter of

[10]J. C. Armington, *Physiological Basis of Psychology*, Dubuque, William C. Brown, 1966, p. 16.

fact, the sixty to seventy pounds of muscle, which include over six hundred in number, attached to the skeleton of the average size man could well be his most important sense organ.

Various estimates indicate that the visual sense brings us upwards of three-fourths of our knowledge. Therefore, it could be said with little reservation that man is "eye-minded." However, it has been reported that a larger portion of the nervous system is devoted to receiving and integrating sensory input originating in the muscles and joint structures than is devoted to the eye and ear combined.[11] In view of this, it could be contended that man is "muscle-sense" minded.

Generally speaking, *proprioception* is concerned with muscle sense. The proprioceptors are sensory nerve terminals that give information concerning movements and position of the body. A proprioceptive feedback mechanism, in a sense, regulates movement. In view of the fact that children are so movement oriented, it appears reasonable to speculate that proprioceptive feedback from the receptors of muscles, skin, and joints contributes in a facilitative manner when the physical education learning medium is used to develop academic skills and concepts. The combination of the psychological factor of motivation and the physiological factor of proprioception, inherent in the physical education learning medium, has caused me to coin the term *motorvation* to describe this phenomenon.

Reinforcement

In considering the compatibility of the physical education learning medium with reinforcement theory, the meaning of reinforcement needs to be taken into account. An acceptable general definition of *reinforcement* would be that there is *an increase in the efficiency of a response to a stimulus brought about by the concurrent action of another stimulus.* The basis for contending that the physical education learning medium is consistent with general reinforcement theory is that this medium reinforces attention to the learning task and learning behavior. It keeps children involved in the learning activity, which is the major area of

---

[11]A. H. Steinhaus, Your muscles see more than your eyes, *Journal of Health, Physical Education, and Recreation,* September 1966.

application for reinforcement procedures. Moreover, there is perhaps little in the way of human behavior that is not reinforced, or at least reinforcible by feedback of some sort, and the importance of proprioceptive feedback has already been discussed in this particular connection.

In summarizing this discussion, it would appear that the physical education learning medium generally establishes a more effective situation for learning reinforcement for the following reasons:

1. The greater motivation of the children in the physical education learning situation involves accentuation of those behaviors directly pertinent to their learning activities, making these salient for the purpose of reinforcement.
2. The prioceptive emphasis in the physical education learning medium involves a greater number of *responses* associated with and conditioned to learning stimuli.
3. The gratifying aspects of the physical education situations provide a generalized situation of *reinforcers*.

Future Prospects of Cognitive Physical Education

Although it is difficult to predict what the future holds for cognitive physical education, I feel assured that more serious attention is currently being paid to it. Discussions with leading neurophysiologists, learning theorists, child-development specialists and others reveal a positive feeling toward the physical education medium of learning; and there is general agreement that the premise is very sound from all standpoints: philosophical, physiological, and psychological. (*Note:* For a detailed account of cognitive physical education the reader is referred to: J. H. Humphrey, *Education of Children Through Motor Activity,* Springfield, Thomas, 1975.)

Chapter Five

PHYSICAL EDUCATION LEARNING ACTIVITIES AND EXPERIENCES

T HE TERMS PHYSICAL EDUCATION *activities* and physical education *experiences* continue to be used interchangeably and oftentimes to mean the same thing. However, it appears advisable to make a clear-cut distinction between these two terms. Physical education activities may be considered as the things children "do" in order to learn, that is, these activities are thought of as learning activities. The term *experience* is defined as *the conscious interaction of the individual with the environment.* Thus, physical education experiences may be considered as the personal feelings that children derive as a result of having engaged in physical education activities. It should be obvious that for ultimate child development to accrue through physical education, those who deal with children should make a concentrated effort to see that physical education activities are selected in such a way that the most desirable and worthwhile learning experiences will result.

CLASSIFICATION OF ACTIVITIES

Any method of classification of activities is arbitrary. The reason, of course, is due to the absence of any kind of standardization of classification systems. The important factor in any method of classification of activities is that the person doing the classifying define precisely his or her meaning of a particular area. The broad classifications I prefer to use for purposes of this book are: (1) basic movement, (2) fundamental skills, (3) game activities, (4) rhythmic activities, and (5) gymnastic activities.

BASIC MOVEMENT

Basic movement as used here implies what most individuals conceive as *movement education*. Whether or not there is a trend for the term *basic movement* to supplant the term *movement education* is certainly open to question. However, well over a decade ago, Dr. Margie R. Hanson, a strong proponent for the so-called movement education approach, indicated that the term basic movement was emerging as the accepted terminology that actually identified the content.[1]

In any event, one of the most important characteristics of life is movement. Whatever else they may involve, practically all of our achievements are based upon our ability to move. Obviously, the very young child is not an intelligent being in the sense of abstract thinking, and he only gradually acquires the ability to deal with symbols and intellectualize his experience in the course of his development. On the other hand, children are creatures of movement and feeling. Any effort to educate a child must take this dominance of movement in the life of the child into account.

For the young child, being able to move as effectively and efficiently as possible is directly related to the proficiency with which he or she will be able to perform the various fundamental motor skills. In turn, the success that children have in physical education activities requiring certain motor skills will be dependent upon their proficiency of performance of these skills. Thus, effective and efficient movement is prerequisite to the performance of basic motor skills needed for success in most physical education activities.

Movement as a Basis for Physical Education

Just as the perception of symbols is concerned with reading readiness, so is basic movement an important factor in readiness to perform in various kinds of physical education activities. Since proficient performance of physical education activities is dependent upon skill of body movement, the ability of the child to move effectively should be readily discerned.

[1]M. R. Hanson, Developing creativity through physical education, presented at the Elementary, Kindergarten, Nursery Education Workshop, St. Paul, June 30, 1967.

Naomi Allenbaugh, Professor Emeritus of the Ohio State University and a modern authority in the area of movement, lends considerable support to this notion.[2] She has maintained that sometimes at a very early age a child may discover and use combinations of movements that in reality are (or will eventuate into) specialized motor skills normally used in the complex organization of a game or dance. In this sense, the child is becoming ready for direct skill teaching and learning. With proper teacher guidance, the basic movements that children develop on their own can be improved in terms of proper principles of body mechanics and commensurate with their natural ability. The important factor is that is the early stages, the child has been made to feel comfortable with the way he moves and, thus, be in a better position to learn correct performance of skills.

Factors Involved in Movement

Generally speaking, in every body movement the following four important factors should be taken into account: (1) time, (2) force, (3) space, and (4) flow.

Time

Time is concerned with how long it takes to complete a movement. For example, a movement can be slow and deliberate, such as a child attempting to create his own body movement to depict a falling snowflake. On the other hand, a movement might be made with sudden quickness, such as starting to run for a goal on a signal.

Force

Force needs to be applied to set the body or one of its segments in motion and to change its speed and/or direction. Thus, force is concerned with how much strength is required for movement. Swinging the arm requires less strength than attempting to propel the body over the surface area with a standing broad jump.

Space

In general, there are two factors concerned with space. These are the amount of space required to perform a particular move-

[2]N. Allenbaugh, Learning about movement. *NEA Journal,* March 1967.

ment and the utilization of available space. With regard to the latter, it has been suggested that young children during nonstructured, self-initiated play seem to reveal differences in the quantity of space they use, and that these differences may be associated in important ways with other aspects of the child's development. Some studies tend to support the concept that space utilization of the young child in active play is a relatively stable dimension of his patterned behavior.

Flow

All movements involve some degree of rhythm in their performance. Thus, flow is the sequence of movement involving rhythmic motion.

The above factors are included in all body movements in various degrees. The degree to which each is used effectively in combination will determine the extent to which the movement is performed with skill.

FUNDAMENTAL SKILLS

Skill is concerned with the degree of proficiency with which a given body movement is performed. This is to say that skills are the scientific way to move the body and/or its segments in such a way as to expend a minimum amount of energy requirement, but achieve maximum results. One prominent neurophysiologist has suggested that skill is the putting together of simple natural movements, of which we have only about two hundred, in unusual or complex combinations to achieve a given objective.[3] Performance of specific skills has been arrived at by scientific insight from such fields as anatomy and kinesiology, which suggests to us how the body can move to achieve maximum efficiency.

Other things being equal, the degree of proficient performance of a skill by any individual is directly related to his or her innate capacity, that is, each individual is endowed with a certain amount of native ability. Through such factors as good teaching, motivation, and the like, attempts are made to help the child per-

---

[3]E. B. Gardner, The neuromuscular base of human movement: feedback mechanisms, *Journal of Health, Physical Education, and Recreation*, October 1965.

form to the best of his or her particular ability and attain the highest *skill level.*

Factors Involved in Skill Teaching and Learning

Because of the importance of the development of certain kinds of motor skills for best performance in physical education activities, one would think that this area of teaching in physical education would receive a great amount of attention. On the contrary, the teaching of physical education skills is one of the most neglected phases of the entire elementary school physical education program. It is indeed a paradoxical situation because the successful performance and resultant enjoyment received from a physical education activity depends in a large measure upon how well the child can perform the elements involved. Yet, at a time in the child's life that is ideal for learning physical education motor skills, we find that in far too many instances this important phase is left almost entirely to chance.

Although each child is born with a certain potential capacity, teachers should not subscribe to the notion that skills are a part of the child's inheritance. Physical education skills must be learned. In order that a child can participate satisfactorily with his peers, he or she must be given the opportunity to learn the skills under careful guidance of competent teachers.

The elementary school has long been considered the educational segment of an individual's life that provides the best opportunity for a solid educational foundation. The need for the development of basic skills in reading, writing, and arithmetic has seldom, if ever, been challenged as an essential purpose of the elementary school. Why, then, should there be a neglect of such an important aspect of learning as that existing in the development of physical education motor skills?

Perhaps the ideal time to learn motor skills is in childhood. The muscular pliability of the young child is such that there is a desirable setting for the acquisition of various kinds of motor skills. The child is at a stage in life when there is a great deal of time for practice—a most important factor because children need practice in order to learn—and at this age level they do not seem to become weary of repeating the same thing over and over again.

In addition, the young child has a limited number of established skills to obstruct the learning of new skills. Skill learning, therefore, should be facilitated provided competent teaching in the area of physical education motor skills is available.

Experimental research on the influence of specific instruction on various kinds of physical education motor skills is somewhat limited. More and more scientific evidence is being accumulated, however, which appears to indicate that children in the early elementary school years are mature enough to benefit by instruction in skills such as throwing and jumping. Unfortunately, this type of instruction is lacking in far too many elementary school physical education programs.

Locomotor Skills

Locomotor skills involve changes in body position that propel the body over the surface area with the impetus being given by the feet and legs. There are five basic types of these skills, namely, walking, running, leaping, jumping, hopping, and three combination skills, which are galloping, skipping, and sliding. The first five of these are performed with an even rhythm, and the last three are done with an uneven rhythm. Locomotor skills require a certain amount of strength and the development of the important sensory-motor mechanisms that are concerned with balance. They also require various degrees of neuromotor coordination for proficient performance.

All of the locomotor skills should be learned by the elementary school-age child. The reason is that these skills comprise the basic requirements for proficiency of performance in the activities contained in a well-planned physical education program for children. Teachers should have certain basic knowledge about the locomotor skills so that they will be alert to improve performance of these skills. The following generalized information is intended for this purpose.

Walking

Walking is the child's first experience with bipedal locomotion. He starts to propel himself over the surface area with uneven, full–sole steps (flatfootedness). He is generally referred to as a "toddler," a term that is perhaps derived from the word "tottering." He appears to be tottering to keep in an upright position, which is indicative of the problems he is having with balance and the force of gravity. At about four years of age, on the average, the child's pattern of walking approximates that of an adult.

Ordinarily, when the child is learning to walk, his only teachers are his family members. Because of this, he is not likely to benefit from instruction on correct procedure. As a result, the very important aspect of foot position is overlooked. Possibly because of this, many children enter school walking in the "toeing out" position rather than pointing the toes straight ahead. Poor walking habits, if allowed to persist, can place undue amounts of strain on certain body parts that in turn may contribute to lack of proficiency in body movement.

Walking involves transferring the weight from one foot to the other. The walk is started with a push-off backward against the surface area with the ball and toes of the foot. After this initial movement the leg swings forward from the hip, the heel of the other foot is placed down, the outer half of the foot next, and then the next push-off is made with toes pointing straight ahead. Walking is used in such physical education activities as walking to rhythmical accompaniment, combining the walk with other movements in various dance activities, walking about in singing games, and walking around a circle preparatory to the start of a circle game activity.

Running

At about eighteen months of age, the average child develops a movement that appears to be in between a walk and a run. This is to say that the walking pattern is accelerated, but does not approximate running form. Usually, it is not before ages five or six that the child's running form becomes similar to that used by an adult. As the child gets older he is able to increase his speed of running as well as be able to run greater distances.

Like walking, running involves transferring the weight from one foot to the other, but the rate of speed is increased. The ball of the foot touches the surface area first, and the toes point straight ahead. The body is momentarily suspended in the air when there is no contact with the surface area. This differs from the walk in which contact with either foot is always maintained with the surface area. In the run, there is more flexion at the knee, which involves a higher leg lift. There is also a higher arm lift, with flexion at the elbow reaching a point of about a right angle. In running, there is more of a forward body lean than in walking, and in both cases the head points straight ahead. In many instances, the child who has not been taught to run correctly will violate certain mechanical principles by having a backward rather than forward lean, by carrying the arms too high, and by turning the head to the side rather than looking straight ahead.

Running is probably the most used of all the locomotor skills in physical education, particularly with most game activities.

Leaping

Leaping, like walking and running, is performed with an even rhythm like a slow run, with one essential difference: the push-off is up and then forward, with the feeling of suspension "up and over." The landing should be on the ball of the foot with sufficient flexion at the knee to absorb the shock.

Although leaping is not used frequently as a specific locomotor skill in many physical education activities, there are certain reasons why it is important that children become proficient in this skill. For example, the leap can be combined with the run to leap over an object so as not to deviate from the running pattern. In addition, in retrieving a ball that has been thrown or hit high, a leap for the ball can help the child catch it "on the run" and thus continue with the running pattern, rather than having to stop his movement.

Specific uses of leaping consist of its performance by children in creative rhythms, where they move as the music makes them feel like moving, or in the case of a game like *Leap the Brook*, the object is to leap over an area while gradually increasing the distance.

Jumping

In a sense, jumping is somewhat like walking and running in that the movement pattern is similar. However, jumping requires elevation of the body off the surface area, and thus more strength is needed to apply force for this purpose. Usually, the child's first experience with a movement approximating jumping occurs when he steps from a higher to a lower level, as in the case of going downstairs. Although there are many variations in the jumping performance of children, generally speaking, they tend to improve their performance as they get older, with improvement tending to be more pronounced for boys than for girls.

Jumping is accomplished by pushing off with both feet and landing on both feet or pushing off with one foot and landing on both feet. Since absorption of shock is important in jumping, the landing should be with flexed knees and on the balls of the feet.

Games such as basketball and volleyball require skill in jumping in order to gain success in such activities. The jump becomes a complete activity in itself when children compete against their own performance in individual jumping. This can be done with the standing broad jump (taking off and landing on both feet) or the long jump (running to a point and taking off on one foot and landing on both feet).

Hopping

While hopping is the least difficult of the "even" rhythmic locomotor skills to describe, at the same time it is perhaps the most difficult to execute. Hopping involves taking off and landing on the same foot. Thus, hopping is a more complex aspect of the jump because the body is elevated from the surface area by the action of only one foot. Not only is greater strength needed for the hop, but also a more refined adjustment of balance is required because of the smaller base of support.

Hopping, as such, is not used frequently as a specific skill in many physical education activities. Exceptions include such dance steps as the schottische, which involves a pattern of "step-step-step-hop-step-hop-step-hop," or the hopping relay in which children hop to a point on one foot and return on the other foot. In addition, it should be obvious that such games as *hopscotch* require skill in the ability to hop.

Even though hopping is not a specific skill used in most physical education activities, one of the more important reasons

why children should become proficient in this locomotor skill is
that it can help them regain balance in any kind of activity where
they have temporarily "lost their footing." When this occurs, the
child can use the hop to keep his balance and remain in an upright
position while getting the temporarily incapacitated foot into
action.

Galloping

The skill of galloping is a combination of the basic patterns of
walking and leaping and is performed with an uneven rhythm.
Since an uneven rhythmic movement requires more neuromotor
coordination, the ability to gallop is developed later than those
locomotor movements requiring an even rhythm. The child is
likely to learn to gallop before he learns to skip, and about one-
half of the children are able to perform at least an approximation
of a galloping movement by about the age of four. Between the
ages of six and seven most children can perform this movement.

Galloping can be explained by pretending that one foot is
injured. A step is taken with the lead foot, but the "injured" foot
can bear very little weight and is brought up only behind the other
one and not beyond it. A transfer of weight is made to the lead
foot, and thus a fast limp is really a gallop.

Galloping is a skill that does not have prevalent use as a specific skill in most physical education activities. One very important exception is its use as a fundamental rhythm when the children become "galloping horses" to appropriate rhythmical accompaniment. One of the most important factors about learning
to gallop is that it helps children to be able to change direction in
a forward or backward plane more easily. Backward galloping
can be done by starting with the lead foot to the back. If a child
is proficient in galloping, he will likely be more successful in game
activities that require a forward and/or backward movement for
successful performance in that particular activity.

Skipping

Although skipping requires more coordination than galloping,
some children will perform variations of the skip around four
years of age. With proper instruction, a majority of children

should be able to accomplish this movement by age six.

Skipping can be taught from the walk. A strong push-off should be emphasized. The push-off should be such a forceful upward one that the foot leaves the surface area. In order to maintain balance a hop is taken. The sequence is step, push-off high, hop. The hop occurs on the same foot that was pushing off, and this is the skip. The two actions cause it to be uneven as to rhythm, with a strong or long action (step) and a short one (hop).

The skill of skipping is rarely used as a specific locomotor skill in many physical education activities. It does find limited use, however, as a fundamental rhythm when children skip to a musical accompaniment, when used in certain singing games and dances, and when skipping around a circle preparatory to the start of certain circle games.

Sliding

Sliding is much the same as the gallop, but movement is in a sideward direction. One foot is drawn up to the lead foot; weight is shifted from the lead foot to the drawing foot and back again. As in the case with the other locomotor skills that are uneven in rhythm, sliding is not used frequently as a specific skill in most physical education activities. The one main exception is its use in many of the social or ballroom dance patterns.

The important feature of gaining proficiency in the skill of sliding is that it helps the child to be able to change direction skillfully in a lateral plane. Many games involving guarding an opponent, such as in basketball, require skill in sliding for success in the game. When a child has developed the skill of sliding from side to side, he does not have to cross his feet and thus can change direction laterally much more easily.

Axial Skills

Axial skills are nonlocomotor in nature. They can be performed with some parts of the body remaining in contact with the surface area or the body as a whole in gross movement. Included among the axial skills are swinging, bending, stretching, pulling, pushing, and the rotation movement of turning and twisting.

Each of these movements are required at one time or another

in the performance of practically all physical education activities. Proficiency of performance of the axial skills will improve performance in locomotor skills; for example, the importance of arm swinging in running. When children can perform the axial skills with grace and facility there is a minimum expenditure of energy, and better performance results.

Auxiliary Skills

There are certain skills that are not ordinarily classified as either locomotor or axial. However, they are most important in the successful performance of most physical education activities. These skills are arbitrarily identified here as auxiliary skills. Among some of the more important of this type of skill are: starting, stopping, dodging, pivoting, falling, and landing.

Starting

In games that require responding to a stimulus, such as running to a goal on the word "go," a quick start is an important contribution to success. How well a child will be able to "start" depends upon his reaction time and speed of movement. Reaction time is the amount of time that it takes from the time a signal is given until the onset of the initial movement. Speed of movement is concerned with how fast the person completes the initial movement. Although the factors concerned with starting are innate, they improve with age and may be improved with practice. When a teacher observes children as being "slow starters," additional help should be given to improve this skill.

Stopping

The skill of stopping is very important because all locomotor movements culminate with this skill. Numerous game activities require quick stopping for successful performance.

Two ways of stopping are the *stride* stop and the *skip* stop. The stride stop involves stopping in running stride. There is flexion at the knees and a slight backward lean to maintain balance. This method of stopping can be used when the performer is moving at a slow speed. The skip stop should be used when there is fast movement, and the performer needs to come to a quick stop. This is accomplished with a hop on either foot, with the other foot making contact with the surface area almost simultaneously. Because of the latter movement, this method of stopping is sometimes called the *jump* stop, because it appears that the performer is landing on both feet at the same time.

Starting and stopping can be practiced in an activity situation with the game *Start and Stop.* In this game, the children are in a straight line with the teacher at the goal line some distance away. The teacher calls "Start," and on this signal all the children run forward. The teacher then calls "Stop," and anyone moving after the signal must return to the starting line. This procedure is continued until one or more children have reached the goal line. The teacher should be alert to detect starting and stopping form.

Dodging

Dodging involves changing body direction while running. The knees are bent, and the weight is transferred in the dodging direction. This movement is sometimes referred to as "veering" or "weaving." After a dodge is made, the performer can continue in the different direction with a push-off from the surface area with the foot to which the weight was previously transferred.

The importance of skill in dodging is seen in game activities where getting away from an opponent (tag games) or an object (dodge ball) is necessary.

Pivoting

Whereas dodging is used to change direction during body movement, pivoting is employed to change direction while the body is stationary. One foot is kept in contact with the surface area, while the other foot is used to push off. A turn is made in the desired direction with the weight on the foot that has maintained contact with the surface area. The angle of the pivot (turn) is determined by the need in the particular situation. This angle is not likely to be over 180 degrees, as might be the case in pivoting away from an opponent in basketball.

Theoretically, the pivot is executed on only one foot; however, a *reverse turn* is sometimes referred to as a "two-foot" pivot. In this case, a complete turn to the opposite direction is made with both feet on the surface area. With one foot ahead of the other, the heels are raised, and a turn is made with the weight equally distributed on both feet.

Pivoting is important in the performance of many kinds of physical education activities, such as various forms of dance and game activities, where quick movements are necessary while the body remains stationary. This is particularly true in games like basketball and speedball where a limited number of steps can be taken while in possession of the ball.

Landing

Landing is concerned with the body coming to the surface area from a height or distance. Absorption when landing is accomplished by bending the knees. The weight is on the balls of the feet, and there is flexion at the ankle and knee joints. After landing, the performer comes to an upright position with the arms in a sideward position so as to keep the body in balance.

Many game activities such as basketball, volleyball, and touch football require the performer to leave the surface area, which makes the skill of landing important. In addition, vaulting over objects in apparatus activities requires skill in landing, not only for good performance, but for safety as well.

Falling

In those activities that require staying in an upright position, emphasis, of course, should be on maintaining this position. Nevertheless, there are occasions when a performer loses balance and falls to the surface area. Whenever possible, a fall should be taken in such a way that injury is least likely to occur. One way to accomplish this is to attempt to "break the fall" with the hands. Relaxation and flexion at the joints that put the performer in a "bunched" position are helpful in avoiding injury when falling to the surface area. Practice of the correct ways to make contact with the surface area when falling can take place in connection with the various rolls in tumbling activities.

Skills of Propulsion and Retrieval

Skills which involve propelling and retrieving objects, in most cases a ball, are used in many types of game activities. It will be the purpose of this section of the book to provide the reader with knowledge of which is important to an understanding of such propelling and retrieving skills as throwing, striking, kicking, and catching.

Throwing

The skill of throwing involves the release of a ball with one or both hands. In general, there are three factors concerned with success in throwing. These are the accuracy or direction of the throw, the distance in which a ball must be thrown, and the amount of force needed to propel the ball.

Any release of an object from the hand or hands could be considered as an act of throwing. Thought of in these terms, the average infant of six months is able to perform a reasonable facsimile of throwing from a sitting position. It has been estimated that by four years of age, about 20 percent of the children show at least a degree of proficiency in throwing. This ability tends to increase rapidly, and between the ages of five and six, over three-fourths of the children can attain a reasonable degree of proficiency as previously defined here.

Sex differences in the early throwing behavior of children tend to favor boys. At all age levels, boys are generally superior to girls in throwing for distance. There is not such a pronounced sex difference in throwing for accuracy, although the performance of boys in this aspect tends to exceed that of girls.

There are generally three accepted throwing patterns. These are the (1) underarm pattern, (2) sidearm pattern, and (3) overarm pattern. It should be noted that although the ball is released by one or both hands, the term "arm" is used in connection with the various patterns. The reason is that the patterns involve a "swing" of the arm.

UNDERARM THROWING PATTERN. The child ordinarily begins the underarm throwing pattern by releasing the ball from both hands. However, he is soon able to release with one hand, especially when the ball is small enough to grip.

At the starting position, the thrower stands facing in the direction of the throw. The feet should be in a parallel position and slightly apart. The right arm is in a position nearly perpendicular to the surface area. (All of the descriptions involving the skills of propulsion and retrieval are for the right-handed child. In the case of the left-handed child, just the opposite should apply.) To start the throw, the right arm is brought back (back swing) to a position where it is about parallel with the surface area. Simultaneously, there is a slight rotation of the body to the right with most of the weight transferred to the right foot. As the arm comes forward (front swing) a step is taken with the left foot. (Stepping out with the opposite foot of the swinging arm is known as the *principle of opposition.*) The ball is released on the front swing when the arm is about parallel with the surface area. During the process of the arm swing, the arm is straight, prescribing a semicircle with no flexion at the elbow. The right foot is carried forward as a part of the follow-through after the release.

The underarm throwing pattern is used in games that involve passing the ball from one person to another over a short distance. It is also used for pitching in the game of softball and other baseball-type games.

SIDEARM THROWING PATTERN. Aside from the direction the thrower faces and the plane of the arm swing, the mechanical principles applied in the sidearm throwing pattern are essentially the same as the underarm throwing pattern.

The thrower faces at a right angle to the direction of the throw, whereas in the underarm throwing pattern he faces in the direction of the throw. The arm is brought to the backswing in a horizontal plane or a position parallel to the surface area. Body rotation and weight shift is the same as in the underarm pattern. The arm remains straight and a semicircle is prescribed from the backswing to the release of the ball on the front swing.

The sidearm throwing pattern will ordinarily be used to propel a ball that is too large to grip with one hand. Thus, on the backswing the opposite hand helps to control the ball until there is sufficient momentum during the swing. Greater distance can be obtained with the sidearm throwing pattern with a ball too large to grip, but accuracy is more difficult to achieve.

OVERARM THROWING PATTERN. Again the basic body mechanics of the overarm throwing pattern are essentially the same as the two previous patterns. The thrower faces in the same direction as for the sidearm throwing pattern, i.e. at a right angle to the direction of the throw. Depending upon individual differences this position may vary. An essential difference in the overarm throwing pattern is the position of the arm. Whereas, in the two previous patterns the arm was kept straight; in the overarm throwing pattern there is flexion at the elbow. Thus, on the backswing the arm is brought back with the elbow bent and with the arm at a right angle away from the body. The arm is then brought forward and the ball is released with a "whiplike" motion at about the height of the shoulder. Foot and arm follow–through is the same as with the underarm and sidearm throwing patterns. This pattern is used for throwing a ball that can be gripped with the fingers in games such as softball where distance as well as accuracy are important.

Striking

Striking involves propelling a ball with a part of the body, ordinarily the hand, as in handball or with an implement such as a bat in softball. The object to be struck can be stationary, e.g batting a ball from a batting tee or moving, e.g. batting a pitched ball in softball.

Some motor development specialists have identified a reasonable facsimile of striking in infancy associated with angry children throwing "nothing" at each other or an adult.

There is some evidence to support the notion that as early as the age of three, verbal direction to children will educe a sidearm striking pattern with a plastic paddle when a tennis ball is suspended in a stationary position at about waist high. In addition, it has been found that at age three, the child will have a degree of success with the sidearm throwing pattern in striking a light ball when tossed slowly to him.[4]

---

[4]L. E. Halverson, and M. A. Robertson, Motor pattern development in young children, *Research Abstracts*, Washington, D.C., American Association for Health, Physical Education and Recreation, 1966.

The principles of body mechanics and the striking patterns are essentially the same as the three previously mentioned throwing patterns—underarm, sidearm, and overarm. The same movements are applied, but in order to propel an object by striking, greater speed is needed with the striking movement. For example, greater speed of movement is needed in the underarm striking pattern when serving a volleyball, than in releasing a ball with a short toss in the underarm throw.

Kicking

Kicking involves propelling a ball with either foot. As early as age two the average child is able to maintain his balance on one foot and propel a stationary ball with the other foot. At this early age the child is likely to have limited action of the kicking foot with little or no follow-through. With advancing age, better balance and strength are maintained that by age six, the child can develop a full leg backswing and a body lean into the kick of a stationary ball.

In kicking, contact with the ball is made with the (1) inside of the foot, (2) outside of the foot, or (3) with the instep of the foot. With the exception of these positions of the foot, the mechanical principles of kicking are essentially the same. The kicking leg is swung back with flexion at the knee. The leg swings forward with the foot making contact with the ball. As in the case of the skill of striking, contact with the ball in kicking can be made when the ball is either stationary or moving.

There is not complete agreement though, in terms of progress in which the skill of kicking is learned. On the basis of personal experience and discussion with successful teachers, I recommend the following sequence.

STATIONARY. The ball and the kicker remain stationary, and the kicker stands beside the ball and kicks it. The kicker is concerned only with the leg movement, and it is more likely that the head will be kept down with the eyes on the ball at the point of contact.

STATIONARY AND RUN. This means that the ball is in a stationary position and that the kicker takes a short run up to the ball before kicking it. This is more difficult, as the kicker must time and coordinate the run to make proper contact with the ball.

KICK FROM HANDS. This is referred to as "punting," as in football and soccer. The ball is dropped from the hands of the kicker, and he takes one or two steps and kicks the ball as it drops. He is kicking a moving ball, but he has control over the movement of the ball before kicking it.

KICKING FROM A PITCHER. This means that another person pitches or rolls the ball to the kicker as in the game of kickball. This is perhaps the most difficult kick because the kicker must kick a moving ball that is under the control of another person.

Catching

Catching with the hands is the most frequently used retrieving skill. One of the child's first experiences with catching occurs at an early stage in life, as when he sits with his legs in a spread position and another person rolls a ball to him. By four years of age, about one-third of the children can retrieve a ball in aerial flight thrown from a short distance. Slightly over half of them can perform this feat by age five, and about two-thirds of them can accomplish this by age six.

There are certain basic mechanical principles that should be taken into account in the skill of catching. It is of importance that the catcher position himself as nearly "in line" with the ball as possible. In this position he will be better able to receive the ball near the center of gravity of the body. Another important factor is hand position. A ball will approach the catcher (1) at the waist, (2) above the waist, or (3) below the waist. When the ball approaches at about waist level, the palms should be facing each other with fingers pointing straight ahead. The "heels" of the hands should be close together depending upon the size of the ball, i.e. closer together for a small ball and farther apart for a large ball. When the ball approaches above the waist, the palms face the ball, and the fingers point upward with the thumbs as close together as necessary. When the ball approaches below the waist, the palms still face the ball but the fingers point downward, with the little fingers as close together as seems necessary, depending again upon the size of the ball. When the ball reaches the hands, it is brought in toward the body, i.e. the catcher "gives" with the catch in order to control the ball and absorb the shock. The position of the feet will likely depend upon the speed with which the ball approaches. Ordinarily, one foot should be in advance of the other in a stride position, with the distance determined by the speed of the approaching ball.

GAME ACTIVITIES

In the last chapter, I gave my description of games as active interactions of children in competitive and/or cooperative situations. This description of games places emphasis on "active" games as opposed to those that are "passive" in nature. This is to say that games in physical education are concerned with a total or near total physical response of children as they interact with each other.

Games not only play a very important part in the school program, but in society in general. The unique quality of games and their application to situations in everyday living have become a part of various colloquial expressions. In many instances, descriptive word phrases from games have become part of their daily vocabulary and appear frequently in news articles and other written material. These words and phrases are used to describe a situation that is so familiar in a game situation that they give a clear meaning to an event from real life.

Many of us have used, at one time or another, the expression "That's the way the ball bounces" to refer to a situation in which the outcome was not as desirable as was anticipated, or, "That's par for the course," meaning that the difficulty was anticipated, and the results were no better or no worse than expected. When we are "home free" we tend to refer to having gotten out of a tight situation, with results better than expected. The expression "The bases are loaded" describes a situation in which a critical point has been reached, and there is much at stake on the next event or series of events. If you have "two strikes against you," you are operating at a grave disadvantage, and if someone "strikes out," he has failed.

It is interesting to consider how the game preferences of a particular country give insight into their culture, and this has been an important area of study and research by sociologists in recent years. The national games, the popular games, and the historical games the people of a nation engage in provide insight into their culture. They are as much a cultural expression as their books, theater, and art.

The physiological value of games has often been extolled because of the vigorous physical nature of many game activities that children participate in. In more recent years, a great deal of credence has been put in the potentialities for modifying human behavior within a social frame of reference, which many games tend to provide. For instance, it has been suggested that the game is probably the child's first social relationship with strangers and his first testing of self against others.

Progression in Games

Essentially, the progression in games is to get the activities in sequence and at the same time aligning it with the progression of difficulty of performance. This is to say that in the same manner as other learning sequences, for example, the arithmetic operations (addition-subtraction-multiplication-division), game activities should progress from the less difficult to the more complex.

There are a variety of different ways in which progression in game activities can be effected, and two such possibilities are considered here. These are: (1) progression of games of the same type, and (2) progression within the same game (modification).

Progression of Games of the Same Type

The games in which the basic objective is essentially the same and yet have so many variations may be considered as a specific type game. Dodgeball is a case in point. Since there are so many versions of dodgeball, these can be considered as games of the dodgeball type. The illustration of this aspect of progression shown here utilizes the games of *Roll Dodge, Circle Dodge,* and *Chain Dodge,* all of which are played in circle formation.

Since there are various ways of organizing dodgeball type games, a comment about organization seems appropriate at this point. The kind of organization that I prefer involves dividing the large group into about four smaller groups. Each small group becomes the "dodgers" for a specified period of time while the other three groups are throwers. Each succeeding small group takes its place as dodgers. Each time a person in the group is hit with the ball, it counts a point against his group, and the group with the lowest score after all four groups have been dodgers is the winner. Organization of this type keeps all of the children in the game all of the time with no one being eliminated.

The game of Roll Dodge has a circle of throwers with a group of dodgers in the circle. Emphasis is placed only upon dodging. The throwers roll the ball back and forth across the surface area as rapidly as they can while the dodgers try to dodge the ball. Children should be encouraged to use the underarm throwing pattern and to release the ball quickly. The previously mentioned method of scoring can be used.

In Circle Dodge, the organization and scoring method is the same as for Roll Dodge. However, the emphasis is placed both upon dodging and attempting to strike a dodger. The ball is thrown rather than rolled, and the children can use either the underarm or sidearm throwing pattern.

In Chain Dodge, the dodgers make a chain by forming a file. Each player gets a firm hold around the waist of the player in front of him. The only person eligible to be hit in the chain is the person at the end of the chain. Any type of throwing pattern can be used. The throwers must move the ball rapidly to each other in various parts of the circle in order to make a hit, and the chain must move in such a way as to protect the person on the end of the chain. If the last person is hit, the game stops temporarily and he goes to the front of the chain, with the previous next-to-last player becoming the player on the end of the chain. The same scoring method prevails.

Progression Within the Same Game (Modification)

Modification of a game means that it is made more or less difficult to meet the needs of a particular group of children. In this case, we would want to make a game increasingly difficult and will use the game of *Call Ball* as an example.

The version of Call Ball used here would require six or more children comprising a circle. One child stands in the center of the circle holding a rubber ball. He tosses the ball into the air and at the same time calls out the name of one of the children. The child whose name is called attempts to catch the ball either on the first bounce or on the fly, depending upon the ability of the children. If the player whose name is called catches the ball, he changes places with the child in the center and the game continues in this manner. If the child whose name is called does not catch the ball, the thrower remains in the center of the circle and tosses the ball up again.

If desired, rather than having a child throw the ball into the air from the center of the circle, the game can be controlled by the teacher's assuming this position. The degree of difficulty in retrieving the ball can be decreased or increased by the number of times the ball bounces. For example, it is easier to retrieve the ball if it is allowed to bounce than if the child is required to catch it on the fly. In addition, if the teacher is the one to put the ball into play, the degree of difficulty in retrieval can be effected by how high or low the ball is thrown into the air. Another way to increase or decrease difficulty is to make the circle of children larger or smaller as desired. The imaginative teacher could have several different combinations of these modifications and thus effect progression of the game within itself.

RHYTHMIC ACTIVITIES

Those human movement experiences that require some sort of rhythmical accompaniment may be placed in the broad category of rhythmic activities. As in the case of defining other terms throughout this text, the definition of rhythmic activities is arbitrary and is used for purposes of discussion here. I am aware that some authorities consider the meaning of the term *dance* to be a broader one than the term *rhythmic activities*. However, the point of view is that there are certain human movement experiences that require some form of rhythmical accompaniment that do not necessarily have the same objectives as those ordinarily associated with dance.

The term *rhythm* is derived from the Greek word *rhythmos,* which means "measured motion." One of the most desirable media for child expression through movement is found in rhythmic activities. One need look only to the functions of the human body to see the importance of rhythm in the life of young children. The heart beats in rhythm, the digestive processes function in rhythm, breathing is done in rhythm; in fact, almost anything in which human beings are involved in is done in a rhythmical pattern.

Status of Rhythmic Activities in Elementary Schools

It is difficult to identify a precise time when rhythmic activities were introduced into the elementary schools of America. Perhaps one of the earlier attempts in this direction came around the turn of the century when John Dewey was director of the University of Chicago Laboratory School. At this time, Dewey had introduced folk dancing into the program, which could possibly be the first time such an activity took place in schools on such a formalized basis. Up until that time, rhythmic activities, if used at all, undoubtedly took place on a sporadic and spasmodic basis. For example, there were instances when certain types of singing games were a part of the "opening exercises" of some elementary schools.

During the decade preceding World War I, some aspects of nationality dances found their way into the school program. This ordinarily occurred in those large cities where certain ethnic backgrounds were predominant in a given neighborhood.

The period between the two world wars saw rhythmic activities introduced into more schools, and this was probably due to the fact that more emphasis was beginning to be placed on the social aspect of physical education. By the late 1920s, some elementary schools were allotting as much as 25 percent of the physical education time to rhythmic activities.

In these modern times, rhythmic activities in elementary schools are characterized by diversity. This aspect of physical education encompasses a wide variety of activities, and there appears to be little standardization from one school to another. Perhaps one of the reasons for this is the variation in teacher preparation and the reluctance on the part of some teachers to teach these kinds of activities.

Classification of Rhythmic Activities

Classification of physical education activities into certain broad categories is a difficult matter. This is partly due to inconsistencies in the use of terminology to describe certain activities. Thus, any attempt at classification tends to become somewhat of an arbitrary matter and is likely to be based upon the experience and personal feelings of the particular person doing the classifying.

When attempts are made to classify activities within a broad category, it should be kept in mind that a certain amount of overlapping is unavoidable and that, in some instances, activities may fit equally well into more than one category. For example, singing games might be classified as either game activities or rhythmic activities. Another important consideration is that in some cases, different names may be given to the same activity, which is concerned with the inconsistencies of terminology mentioned previously. For example, "creative rhythms" and "free-response rhythms" might be considered one and the same.

One approach to the classification of rhythmic activities centers around the kinds of *rhythmic experiences* that one might wish children to have. It is recommended here that these experiences consist of (1) unstructured experiences, (2) semistructured experiences, and (3) structured experiences. It should be understood that in this particular way of grouping rhythmic experiences a certain amount of overlapping will occur as far as the degree of structuring is concerned, that is, although an experience is classified as an unstructured one, there could possibly be some small degree of structuring in certain kinds of situations. With this idea in mind the following descriptions of these three types of rhythmic experiences are submitted.

Unstructured experiences include those where there is an original or creative response and in which there has been little, if any, previous explanation or discussion in the form of specified directions. The *semistructured experiences* include those certain movements or interpretations suggested by the teacher, child, or a group of children. *Structured experiences* involve the more difficult rhythmic patterns associated with various types of dances. A well-balanced program of rhythmic activities for children should provide opportunities for these various types of rhythmic experiences. An arbitrary classification of rhythmic activities designed to provide such experiences for children gives consideration to (1) fundamental rhythms, (2) creative rhythms, (3) singing games, and (4) dances.

At the primary level, *fundamental rhythmic activities* found in the locomotor movements of walking, running, jumping, hopping, leaping, skipping, galloping, and sliding, and the nonlocomotor or axial movements, such as twisting, turning, and stretching, form the basis for all types of rhythmic patterns. Once the children have developed skill in the fundamental rhythms, they are ready to engage in some of the more complex dance patterns. For example, the combination of walking and hopping to musical accompaniment is the basic movement in the aforementioned dance known as the schottische. In a like manner, galloping is related to the basic pattern used in the polka.

Children at the primary level should be given numerous opportunities to engage in *creative rhythms*. This kind of rhythmic activity helps them to express themselves in just the way the accompaniment "makes them feel" and gives vent to expression so necessary in the life of the child.

The *singing game* is a rhythmic activity suitable for primary age children. In this type of activity, children can sing their own accompaniment for the various activity patterns that they use in performing the singing game.

Various kinds of *dances* may be included as a part of the program of rhythmic activities for the primary level. Ordinarily, these have simple movement patterns the child may learn before progressing to some of the more complex patterns. At the upper elementary level, children can engage in rhythmic activities that are more advanced than those at the primary level. Creative rhythms should be continued, and children should have the opportunity to create more advanced movement patterns.

Dance patterns involved in the various kinds of folk dances may be somewhat more complex, provided children have had a thorough background in fundamental rhythms and less complicated folk dances at the primary level. Primary level dances can be individual activities and many of them involve dancing with a partner. At the upper elementary level, "couple dances," which require closer coordination of movement by partners, may be introduced.

Some of the forms of American square dancing are ordinarily introduced at the upper elementary level, although many teachers have had successful experience with square dancing at the lower grade levels.

GYMNASTIC ACTIVITIES*

In recent years a number of modifiers have been used with the term *gymnastics*. Included among these are "artistic" gymnastics, "competitive" gymnastics, "olympic" gymnastics, and "educational" gymnastics. The latter term seems to be preferred because it "focuses on gymnastics within the school program where every child is provided with equal opportunities to learn."[5] However, I would like to emphasize that "educational gymnastics" is not a new term. On the contrary, it first came into use before the turn of the century to differentiate between those gymnastics which adhered to the principles of education from "hygienic" gymnastics to be used for therapeutic purposes.

Certain physical education activities that are based upon the child's desire to compete against himself and natural forces may be placed in the category of gymnastic activities. Activities such as stunts and tumbling, and exercises with or without apparatus, can be classified in this category.

With regard to stunts and tumbling it should be mentioned that these activities are closely related and alike. Stunts are concerned predominantly with certain kinds of imitations and the performance of a variety of kinds of feats that utilize such abilities as balance, coordination, flexibility, ability, and strength. Tumbling involves various kinds of body rolls and body springs that en-

---

*In the past, I have tended to use the term *self-testing activities,* which is broader in scope. This includes fundamental skills as well as gymnastic activities, however, for reasons previously given, I have considered fundamental skills as a separate classification.

[5] S. A. Parent, Educational gymnastics, *Journal of Physical Education and Recreation,* September 1978.

courages the development of these same abilities.

At the primary level, children should be given the opportunity to participate in gymnastic activities commensurate with their ability. For example, stunts that involve imitations of animals are of great interest to boys and girls at this age level. Tumbling activities using some of the simple rolls are suitable. Simple apparatus activities utilizing such equipment as ladders, bars, and balance beams are very popular.

Gymnastic activities at the upper elementary level should be somewhat more advanced provided the child has had previous experience and teaching in them at the primary level. Tumbling activities that involve more advanced rolls and various kinds of body springs may be successfully introduced. In a like manner, more difficult kinds of balance stands may be used in the stunt program. Children at the upper elementary level may continue to take part in apparatus activities using much the same equipment that was used for the primary level, but moving to more advanced skills.

One of the major values ordinarily attributed to gymnastic activities is their specific contribution to such elements of physical fitness as strength, agility, coordination, and flexibility. Zealous proponents of gymnastic activities stoutly maintain that contributions to these various factors are more likely to accrue through gymnastic activities than may be the case through games and rhythmic activities. The reason for this lies in the fact that successful performance of certain gymnastic activities requires the employment of the various elements of physical fitness.

It has also been suggested by many teachers that some of these kinds of activities help to build courage, confidence, and poise in children, although this is difficult to evaluate objectively.

Chapter Six

THE ROLE OF THE TEACHER

THE FOCAL point of any teaching-learning situation is the teacher. Frequently, a communication medium appears that is heralded not only as a teaching aid, but as a teacher substitute as well. The enormous expense of mass education, coupled with the need for high-quality teaching, has given rise to the wish that somehow a relatively few master teachers could direct the learning of large numbers of persons. In this way, it has been reasoned, both quantitative and qualitative problems of American education could be solved or at least minimized.

Several of the mass media of communication have been proposed with varying degrees of enthusiasm as the answer to this problem of educating large numbers of children well. Recordings, radio, films, television, teaching machines, and other mechanical and technical devices have been experimented with and widely used. In spite of their great value in education, all the mass media of communication have been found wanting when tried as teacher "substitutes" rather than as teaching "aids," perhaps especially at the elementary school level. It is interesting to consider why.

In brief, the answer probably lies in the fact that although a teacher usually deals with a group of children, he or she must remain sensitive to the individual. The qualified teacher is aware that every child is almost incredibly unique and that he approaches all learning tasks with his own level of motivation, capacity, experience, and vitality. Moreover, such a teacher is aware that the individuals in a class must be prepared for a learning experience so that the experience may, in some way, be recognized by them as having meaning for them. Preparation of any class must be in terms of the particular individuals in that class.

The teacher must then, by a combination of emotional and logical appeal, help each individual find his way through the experience at his own rate and, to some extent, in his own way. The teacher must also help the individual "nail down" the meaning of the experience to himself and help him to incorporate it and its use into his own life. The point of view reflected here is that there is no substitute for a competent teacher who, while necessarily teaching a group, is highly sensitive to the individual children involved.

The role of the teacher in providing physical education learning experiences for children differs little than in other teaching-learning situations. The essential difference is that the teacher deals with the children in movement experiences, while in the other subject matter areas the learning activities are more or less sedentary in nature.

The teacher's role should be that of a guide who supervises and directs desirable physical education learning experiences. In providing such experiences, the teacher should constantly keep in mind how physical education can contribute to the physical, social, emotional, and intellectual development of every child. This implies that the teacher should develop an understanding of principles of learning and attempt to apply these principles properly in the teaching of physical education.

It is important the teacher recognize that individual differences exist among teachers as well as children and that some of these differences will influence their teaching method. Sometimes one teacher may have greater success than another with a method. This implies that there should be no specified resolute method of teaching for all teachers. On the other hand, teachers should allow themselves to deviate from recommended conformity if they are able to provide desirable learning experiences through a method peculiar to their own abilities. This, of course, means that the procedures used should be compatible with conditions under which learning takes place best.

CHARACTERISTICS OF GOOD TEACHERS

Over the years there have been numerous attempts to identify objectively those characteristics of good teachers that set them apart from average or poor teachers. Obviously, this is a difficult matter because of the countless variables involved.

It is entirely possible for two teachers to possess the same degree of intelligence, preparation, and understanding of the subject they teach. Yet, it is also possible that one of these teachers will consistently achieve good results with children, while the other will not have much success. Perhaps a good part of the reason for this difference in success lies in those individual differences of teachers that relate to certain personality factors and how they deal and interact with children. Based upon the available research and numerous interviews with both teachers and children, I have found that the following characteristics tend to emerge most often among good teachers.

1. Good teachers possess those characteristics that in one way or another have a humanizing effect on children. An important factor of good teachers that appeals to most children is a sense of humor. One third grade child put it this way, "She laughed when we played a joke on her."
2. In all cases, good teachers are fair and democratic in their dealings with children and tend to maintain the same positive feelings toward the so-called "problem" child as they do with other children.
3. Another very important characteristic is that good teachers are able to relate easily to children. They have the ability and sensitivity to "listen through children's ears and see through children's eyes."
4. Good teachers are flexible. They know that different approaches need to be used with different groups of children as well as individual children. In addition, good teachers can adjust easily to changing situations.
5. Good teachers are creative. This is an extremely important factor, because in movement experiences at the elementary school level teachers are dealing with a very imaginative segment of the population.
6. Good teachers have control. Different teachers exercise control in different ways, but good teachers tend to have a minimum of control problems probably because they provide a learning environment where control becomes a minimum problem.

TEACHING AND LEARNING IN PHYSICAL EDUCATION

The teaching-learning process is complicated and complex. For this reason it is important that teachers have as full an understanding as possible of the role of teaching and learning in elementary school physical education.

Basic Considerations

The concepts of learning that an individual teacher or a group of teachers in a given school subscribe to are directly related to the kind and variety of physical education learning activities and experiences that will be provided for children. For this reason it is important for teachers to explore some of the factors that makes for the most desirable and worthwhile learning. Among the factors that should help to orient the reader with regard to some basic understandings in the teaching of physical education are (1) an understanding of the meaning of certain terms, (2) an understanding of the derivation of teaching methods, and (3) an understanding of the various learning products in physical education.

Meaning of Terms

Due to the fact that certain terms, because of their multiple use, do not actually have a universal definition, no attempt will be made here to define terms. On the other hand, it will be the purpose to describe certain terms rather than attempt to define them. The reader should view the descriptions of terms that follow with this general idea in mind.

LEARNING. Without exception, most definitions of learning are characterized by the idea that learning involves some sort of change in the individual. This means that when an individual has learned, behavior is modified in one or more ways. Thus, a valid criterion for learning would be that after having an experience, a person could behave in a way in which he could not have behaved before having had the experience. In this general connection, many learning theorists suggest that it is not possible to "see" learning. However, behavior can be seen, and when a change in behavior has occurred, then it is possible to infer that change and learning have occurred.

TEACHING.   Several years ago I was addressing a group of
teachers on the subject of teaching and learning. Introducing the
discussion in somewhat abstract terms, I asked, "What is teaching?" After a short period of embarrassing deliberation, one member of the group interrogated the following answer with some degree of uncertainty: "Is it imparting information?" This kind
of thinking is characteristic of that which reflects the traditional
meaning of the term "teaching." A more acceptable description of
teaching would be to think of it in terms of guidance, direction,
and supervision of behavior that results in desirable and worthwhile learning. This is to say that it is the job of the teacher to
guide the child's learning rather than to impart to him a series of
unrelated and sometimes meaningless facts.
METHOD.   The term "method" might be considered as an
orderly and systematic means of achieving an objective. In other
words, method is concerned with "how to do" something in order
to achieve desired results. If best results are to be obtained for
elementary school children through physical education, it becomes
necessary that the most desirable physical education learning experiences be provided. Consequently, it becomes essential that
teachers use all of the ingenuity and resourcefulness at their com-
mand in the proper direction and guidance of these learning experiences. The procedures that teachers use are known as *teaching
methods*.

Derivation of Teaching Methods

Beginning teachers often ask, "Where do we get our ideas for
teaching methods?" For the most part this question should be
considered in general terms. In other words, although there are
a variety of acceptable teaching procedures utilized in the modern
elementary school, all of these methods are likely to be derived
from two somewhat broad sources.

The first of these involves an accumulation of knowledge of
educational psychology and what is known about the learning
process in providing physical education learning experiences.
The other is the practice of successful teachers.

In most instances, undergraduate preparation of prospective
teachers includes at least some study of educational psychology as

it applies to the learning process and certain accepted principles of learning. With this basic information it is expected that beginning teachers have sufficient knowledge to make application of it to the practical situation.

It has been my observation over a period of years that many beginning teachers tend to rely too much upon the practices of successful teachers as a source of teaching methods. The validity of this procedure is based on the assumption that such successful practices are likely to have as their bases the application of fundamental psychological principles of learning. Nevertheless, it should be the responsibility of every teacher to become familiar with the basic psychological principles of learning and to attempt to apply these in the best possible way when providing the most desirable and worthwhile physical education learning experiences for children.

Learning Products in Physical Education

In general, three learning products can be identified that accrue from participation in physical education activities, namely, direct, incidental, and indirect. In a well-planned program, these learning products should develop satisfactorily through physical education activities.

Direct learning products are those that are the direct object of teaching. For instance, running, dodging, jumping, throwing, and catching are some of the important skills necessary for reasonable degrees of proficiency in the game of dodgeball. Through the learning of skills, more enjoyment is derived from participating in an activity than just the practice of the skills. For this reason, the learning of skills is one of the primary direct objects of teaching. However, it should be understood that certain incidental and indirect learning products can result from direct teaching in physical education. The zeal of a participant to become a more proficient performer gives rise to certain incidental learning products. These may be inherent in the realization and acceptance of practices of healthful living, which make the individual a more skilled performer in the activity.

Attitudes have often been considered in terms of behavior tendencies and as such might well be concerned with indirect learning products. This type of learning product involves such qualities as sportsmanship, appreciation of certain aspects of the activity, and other factors that involve the adjustment and modification of the individual's reactions to others.

Teachers who have the responsibility for providing physical education programs for children should give a great deal of consideration to these various kinds of learning products. This is particularly important if children are to receive the full benefit of the many physical education learning experiences that should be provided for them.

SOME PRINCIPLES OF LEARNING APPLIED TO PHYSICAL EDUCATION

There are various basic facts about the nature of human beings of which modern educators are more cognizant than educators of the past. Essentially, these facts involve some of the fundamental aspects of the learning process, which all good teaching should take into account. Older concepts of teaching methods were based largely upon the idea that the teacher was the sole authority in terms of what was best for children, and that children were expected to learn regardless of the conditions surrounding the learning situation. For the most part, modern teaching replaces the older concepts with methods that are based on certain accepted beliefs of educational psychology. Outgrowths of these beliefs emerge in the form of principles of learning. The following principles provide important guidelines for arranging learning experiences for children, and they suggest how desirable learning can take place when the principles are satisfactorily applied to physical education.

1. THE CHILD'S OWN PURPOSEFUL GOALS SHOULD GUIDE HIS LEARNING ACTIVITIES. In order for a desirable learning situation to prevail, teachers must consider certain features about purposeful goals which guide learning activities. Of utmost importance is the fact that the goal must seem worthwhile to the child. This will perhaps involve such factors as interest, attention, and motivation. Fortunately, in the recommended activities from which physical education learning experiences are drawn, interest, attention, and motivation are likely to be inherent qualities. Thus,

the teacher does not always necessarily need to "arouse" the child with various kinds of motivating situations. On the other hand, the type of program that has body conditioning as its only objective may take a great deal of coercing on the part of the teacher to induce participation. In other words, engaging in a variety of "setting-up" exercises may not seem to be a worthwhile goal to the child.

The goal should not be too difficult for the child to achieve. While it should present a challenge, it should be something that is commensurate with his abilities and within his realm of achievement. By the same token, the goal should not be too easy or it will not be likely that the child will have the opportunity to develop to his greatest possible capacity. To be purposeful, a goal should give direction to activity and learning. In substance, this implies that after a child has accepted a goal he should have a better idea of where he is going and what he should be able to accomplish in a given situation.

It is important that the child find, adopt, and accept his own goals. This implies that he should not receive them directly from the teacher. If the most desirable learning is to take place, it is doubtful if one person can give another person a goal. This should not be interpreted to mean that goals may not originate with the teacher. On the contrary, the teacher can be of considerable help in assisting children to find their own goals. This can be done by planning the physical education learning environment in such a way that children with varying interests and abilities may find something that appears to be worthwhile. This procedure can be followed and still be in keeping with the teacher's objectives. For instance, it may be a goal of the teacher to improve the social relationships of children in a given physical education class. This might be accomplished by providing a variety of gymnastic activities with children participating in groups and requiring that each member of the group achieve a certain degree of proficiency in a given activity before the entire group is given credit for achievement. Experience has shown that this procedure has been most useful in welding together a group of children who have previously experienced some difficulty in getting along together. While the goal of obtaining better social relationships originated with the teacher, the experience was planned in such a way that the goal was eventually adopted by the children.

2. THE CHILD SHOULD BE GIVEN SUFFICIENT FREEDOM TO CREATE HIS OWN RESPONSES IN THE SITUATION HE FACES. This principle indicates that *problem solving* is a very important way of human learning and that the child will learn largely only through experience, either direct or indirect. This implies that the teacher should provide every opportunity for children to utilize judgment in the various situations that arise in physical education activities.

It should be borne in mind that although the child learns through experience, this does not mean that experience will assure desirable learning, since it might possibly come too soon. For example, children at the first-grade level are not expected to learn some of the complex skill patterns involved in the highly organized game of basketball, simply because at that level they are not ready for it.

When children are free to create their own responses in the situation they face, individual differences are being taken into consideration, and, generally, experience comes at the right time for desirable learning. This situation necessitates an activity area environment flexible to the extent that children can achieve in relation to their individual abilities.

In a sense, this principle of learning refutes, and perhaps rightly so, the idea that there is a specific "problem-solving method" mutually exclusive from other methods. In other words, all methods should involve problem solving, which actually means the application of this principle.

3. THE CHILD AGREES TO AND ACTS UPON THE LEARNING WHICH HE CONSIDERS OF MOST VALUE TO HIM. Children accept as most valuable those things that are of greatest interest to them. This principle implies in part, then, that there should be a satisfactory balance between *needs* and *interests* of children as criteria for the selection of physical education activities. Although it is of extreme importance to consider the needs of children in developing experiences, the teacher should not lose sight of the fact that their interest is needed if the most desirable learning is to take place.

While needs and interests of children may be closely related, there are nevertheless differences that should be taken into consideration when physical education learning activities are selected. Interests are mostly acquired as products of the environment, while needs, particularly those of an individual nature, are more likely to be innate. Herein lies one of the main differences in the two criteria insomuch as the selection of physical education learning activities is implicated. For instance, a child may demonstrate a temporary interest in an activity that may not contribute to his needs at a certain age level. This interest may be aroused because of the child's environment. Perhaps an older brother, sister, or a parent may influence a child to develop an interest in an activity that would not contribute to his needs or possibly have a detrimental effect on him. Despite the inevitability of such contingencies, interests of children may serve as one of the valid criteria for the selection of physical education learning activities. In this connection it is interesting to note that there is a rather marked relationship between physical education learning activities—recommended by experts in the field of physical education—and child interest in these same activities.

To a certain extent, interests may be dependent upon past experiences of children. For instance, interests in certain physical education activities may stem from the fact that they are a part of the traditional background of the community and as such have absorbed the interest of parents as well as children.

4. THE CHILD SHOULD BE GIVEN THE OPPORTUNITY TO SHARE COOPERATIVELY IN LEARNING EXPERIENCES WITH HIS CLASSMATES UNDER THE GUIDANCE, BUT NOT THE CONTROL OF THE TEACHER. The point that should be emphasized here is that although learning may be an individual matter, it is likely to take place best in a group. This is to say that children learn individually, but that socialization should be retained. Moreover, sharing in group activities seems absolutely essential in educating for democracy.

The physical education situation should present near-ideal conditions for a desirable balance between individualization and socialization. For example, the elements of an activity must be learned individually, but then they are combined by the entire group in a game situation. In a game, each child learns how to perform the skills necessary for successful performance in the game situation. However, he may improve his skill or application of skill when he is placed in the actual game situation. Another example may be seen in the performance of certain gymnastic activities. Although these are predominantly individual in nature, children oftentimes work together in small groups assisting each other and, as a consequence, are likely to learn from each other by pooling and sharing experience.

5. THE TEACHER SHOULD ACT AS A GUIDE WHO UNDERSTANDS THE CHILD AS A GROWING ORGANISM. This principle indicates that the teacher should consider learning as an evolving process and not just as instantaneous behavior. If teaching is to be regarded as the guidance and direction of behavior which results in learning, the teacher must display wisdom as to when to "step in and teach" and when to step aside and watch for further opportunities to guide and direct behavior.

The application of this principle precludes an approach of teacher domination. On the other hand, the implementation of this principle is perhaps more likely to be realized in physical education classes where the teacher recognizes that numerous problem-solving situations are inherent in many physical education situations. For example, if a particular activity is not going as it should, the teacher can stop the activity and evaluate it with the children so that they can determine how the activity may be improved. In other words, children are placed in a position to identify problems connected with the activity and given the opportunity to exercise judgment in solving them. The teacher thus helps the children discover direct pathways to meaningful areas of experience and at the same time contributes to the children's ability to become self-directed individuals.

PHASES OF THE TEACHING-LEARNING SITUATION

There are certain fundamental phases involved in almost every physical education teaching-learning situation. These are (1) auditory input, (2) visual input, (3) participation, and (4) evaluation. Although these four phases are likely to be weighted in various degrees, they will occur in the teaching of practically every physical education lesson regardless of the type of activity that is being taught. While the application of the various phases may be of a general nature, they nevertheless should be utilized in such a way that they become specific in a particular situation. Depending upon the type of activity being taught—game, rhythm, or gymnastic activity—the use and application of the various phases should be characterized by flexibility and awareness of the objectives of the lesson.

Auditory-Input Phase

The term *auditory* may be described as stimulation occurring through the sense organs of hearing. In education, the term *input* is concerned with the use of as many media as are deemed necessary for a particular teaching-learning situation. The term *output* is concerned with behaviors or reactions of the learner resulting from the various forms of input. Auditory input involves the various learning media that are directed to the auditory sense. This should not be interpreted to mean that the auditory-input phase of the teaching-learning situation is a one-way process. While much of such input may originate with the teacher, consideration should also be given to the verbal interaction among children and between the children and the teacher.

Physical education provides a most desirable opportunity for learning through direct, purposeful experience. In other words, the physical education learning situation is "learning by doing," or learning through pleasurable physical acitvity. Although verbalization might well be kept to a minimum, a certain amount of auditory input, which should provide for auditory-motor association, appears to be essential for a satisfactory teaching-learning situation. The quality of "kinesthetic feel" may be described as the process of changing ideas into muscular action and is of primary importance in the proper acquisition of physical education motor skills. It might be said that the auditory-input phase of teaching helps to set the stage for a kinesthetic concept of the particular activity being taught.

Listening experiences are, no doubt, among the most abstract of the learning media used with children. As such, this type of learning experience has been much maligned by some educators. However, it should be pointed out that the child first learns to act on the basis of verbal instructions by others. In this regard, it has been suggested that later on he learns to guide and direct his own behavior on the basis of his language activities; he literally talks to himself and gives himself instructions.

This point of view is supported by research, which has postulated that speech as a form of communication between children and adults later becomes a means of organizing the child's own behavior. The function that was previously divided between two people—child and adult—later becomes an internal function of human behavior.

Great care should be taken with the auditory-input phase in the physical education teaching-learning situation. The ensuing discussions are intended to suggest to the reader ways in which the greatest benefits can accrue when using this particular learning medium.

Preparing the Children for Listening

Since it is likely that the initial part of the auditory-input phase will originate with the teacher, care should be taken to prepare the children for listening. The teacher may set the scene for listening by relating the activity to the interests of the children. In addition, the teacher should be on the alert to help children develop their own purposes for listening.

In preparing children to listen, the teacher should be aware that it is of importance that the comfort of the children be taken into consideration and that attempts should be made for removing any possible attention-distracting factors. Although evidence concerning the effect of environmental distractions on listening effectiveness is not in great abundance, there is reason to believe that distraction does interfere with listening comprehension. Moreover, it was reported years ago that being able to see as well as hear the speaker is an important factor in listening distraction.

These factors have a variety of implications for the auditory-input phase of the physical education teaching-learning situation. For example, consideration should be given to the placement of children when a physical education activity requires auditory input by the teacher. This means, for instance, that if the teacher is providing auditory input from a circle formation, the teacher should take a position as part of the circle instead of speaking from the center of the circle. Also, it might be well for teachers to consider that an object, such as a ball, can become an attention-distracting factor when an activity is being discussed. The attention of children is sometimes focused on the ball, and they may not listen to what is being said. The teacher might wish to conceal such an object until time for its use is most appropriate. With reference to the importance of the listener being able to see the speaker, teachers might exercise caution in the use of records for rhythmic activities which include instructions on the record. Particularly with primary level children it might be well for the teacher to use the instructions only for himself or herself and the musical accompaniment for the children.

Teacher-Child and Child-Child Interaction

It was mentioned previously that the auditory-input phase is a two-way process. As such, it is important to take into account certain factors involving verbal interaction of children with children, and teacher with children.

By "democracy" some people seem to mean everyone doing or saying whatever happens to cross his mind at the moment. This raises the question of control, and it should be emphasized that group discussions, if they are to be democratic, must be in control. This is to say that if a group discussion is to succeed it must be under control, and let me stress that democracy implies discipline and control.

Group discussion is a kind of sociointellectual exercise (involving numerous bodily movements, of course) just as basketball is a kind of sociointellectual exercise (involving, too, higher mental functioning). Both imply individual discipline to keep play moving within bounds, and both require moderators (or officials) overseeing, though not participating in, the play in a manner that is objective and aloof from the heat of competition. In brief, disciplined, controlled group discussion can be a training ground for living in a society in which both individual and group interests are profoundly respected—just as games can serve a comparable function.

Another important function in teacher-child verbal interaction is with the time given to questions after the teacher has provided auditory input. The teacher should give time for questions from the group, but should be very skillful in the use of questions. It must be determined immediately whether or not a question is a legitimate one. This implies that the type of questions asked can help to serve as criteria for the teacher to evaluate the auditory-input phase of teaching. For example, if numerous questions are asked, it is apparent that either the auditory input from the teacher was unsatisfactory or the children were not paying attention.

Directionality of Sound

In summarizing recent findings concerned with the directionality of sound, Smith has pointed up a number of interesting factors important to the auditory-input phase.[1] She mentions that individuals tend to initiate movements toward the direction from which the sound cue emanates. For example, if a verbal cue is given that instructs the individual to move a body segment or segments to the left, but the verbal cue emanates from the right side of the individual, the initial motor response is to the right, followed by a reverse response to the left. Emphasizing the importance of this, Smith recommends that when working on direction of motor responses with young children, one should make certain that sound cues come from the direction in which the motor response is made. The point is made that children have enough difficulty in discriminating left from right without confounding them further.

Visual-Input Phase

The term *visual* is concerned with images that are obtained through the eyes. Thus, visual input involves the various learning media which are directed to the visual sense.

Various estimates indicate that the visual sense brings us upwards of three-fourths of our knowledge. If this postulation can be used as a valid criterion, the merits of the visual-input phase in teaching physical education are readily discernible. In many

[1]H. M. Smith, Implications for movement education experiences drawn from perceptual-motor research, *Journal of Health, Physical Education and Recreation,* April 1970.

cases, visual input, which should provide for visual-motor association, serves as a happy medium between verbal symbols and direct participation in helping teachers further to prepare children for the kinesthetic feel mentioned previously.

In general, there are two types of visual input which can be used satisfactorily in teaching physical education. These are visual symbols and human demonstration (live performance).

Visual Symbols

Included among the visual symbols used in physical education are motion pictures and various kinds of flat or still pictures. One of the disadvantages of the latter centers around the difficulty in portraying movement with a still figure. Although movement is obtained with a motion picture, it is not depicted in third dimension, which causes some degree of ineffectiveness when this medium is used. One valuable use of visual symbols is that of employing diagrams to show the dimensions of activity areas. This procedure may be useful when the teacher is discussing an activity in the room before going on to the outdoor activity area. Court dimensions and the like can be diagramed on a chalkboard, providing a good opportunity for integration with other areas such as mathematics and drawing to scale.

Human Demonstration

Some of the guides to action in the use of demonstration follow:

1. If the teacher plans to demonstrate, this should be included in the preparation of the lesson by practicing and rehearsing the demonstration.
2. The teacher does not need to do all the demonstrating; in fact, in some cases it may be much more effective to have one or more children demonstrate. Since the teacher is expected to be a skilled performer, a demonstration by a child will oftentimes serve to show other children that one of their peers can perform the activity and that they should be able to do it also.
3. A demonstration should be based on the skill and ability of a given group of children. If it appears to be too difficult

for them, they might not want to attempt the activity.

4. When at all possible, a demonstration should parallel the timing and conditions of when it will be put to practical application. However, if the situation is one in which the movements are complex or done with great speed, it might be well to have the demonstration conducted on a slower basis than that involved in the actual performance situation.

5. The group should be arranged so that everyone is in a favorable position to see the demonstration. Moreover, the children should be able to view the demonstration from a position where it takes place. For example, if the activity is to be performed in a lateral plane, children should be placed so that they can see it from this position.

6. Although auditory input and human demonstration can be satisfactorily combined in many situations, care should be taken that auditory input is not lost, because the visual sense offsets the auditory sense, that is, one should not become an attention-distracting factor for the other. It will be up to the teacher to determine the amount of verbalization that should accompany the demonstration.

7. After the demonstration has been presented it may be a good practice to demonstrate again and have the children go through the movements with the demonstrator. This provides for the use of the kinesthetic sense together with the visual sense that makes for close integration of these two sensory stimuli.

Participation Phase

Direct, purposeful experience is the foundation of all education. Because physical education activities are motor in character, there is a near-ideal situation for learning in this particular area of the elementary school curriculum. The child needs to get his hands on the ball, feel his body coordinated in the performance of a stunt, or dance the folk dance in order to gain a full appreciation of the activity. There is an opportunity in a well-taught physical education lesson for learning to become a part of the child's physical reality, providing for a pleasurable concrete experience, rather than an abstract one. For this reason the following considerations should be kept in mind in connection with the participation phase of teaching.

1. The class period should be planned so that the greatest possible amount of time is given to participation.
2. If the activity does not progress as expected in the participation phase, perhaps the fault may lie in the procedures used in the auditory- and visual-input phases. Participation then becomes a criterion for the evaluation of former phases.
3. The teacher should take into account the fact that the original attempts in learning an activity should meet with a reasonable degree of success.
4. The teacher should constantly be aware of the possibility of fatigue of children during participation and should understand that individual differences in children create a variation with regard to how rapidly fatigue takes place.
5. Participation should be worthwhile for every child, and all children should have the opportunity to achieve. Procedures which call for elimination of participants should be avoided lest some individuals do not receive the full value from participation.
6. The teacher should be ever on the alert to guide and direct learning, thus making the physical education period a teaching learning period.
7. During the participation phase, the teacher should constantly analyze performance of children in order to determine those who need improvement in skills. Behaviorisms of children should be observed while they are engaging in physical education activities. For example, various types of emotional behavior might be noted in game situations that might not be indicated in any other school activity.
8. Problems involved during participation should be kept in mind for subsequent evaluation of the lesson with the children.

Evaluation Phase

Evaluation is a very important phase of the physical education teaching-learning situation, and, yet, perhaps one of the most neglected aspects of it. For instance, it is not an uncommon procedure to have the physical education class period end at the signal of the bell, with the children hurrying and scurrying from the activity area without an evaluation of the results of the lesson.

Children should be given the opportunity to discuss the lesson and to suggest ways in which improvement might be effected. When this procedure is followed, children are placed in a problem-solving situation and desirable learning is more likely, with the teacher guiding learning rather than dominating the situation in a direction-giving type of procedure. Also, more and better continuity is likely to be provided from one lesson to another when time is taken for evaluation. In addition, children are much more likely to develop a clearer understanding of the purposes of physical education if they are given an opportunity to discuss the procedures involved in the lesson.

Ordinarily, the evaluation phase should take place at the end of the lesson. Experience has shown that a satisfactory evaluation procedure can be effected in three to six minutes, depending upon the nature of the activity and upon what actually occurred during a given lesson. Under certain circumstances, if an activity is not proceeding well in the participation phase, it may be desirable to stop the activity and carry out what is known as a "spot" evaluation. This does not mean that the teacher should stop an activity every time the situation is not developing according to plan. A suggestion or a hint to children who are having difficulty with performance can perhaps preclude the need for having all of the children cease participation. On the other hand, if the situation is such that the needs of the group will best be met by a discussion concerning the solution of a problem, the teacher is indeed justified in stopping the activity and conducting an evaluation "on the spot."

Teachers should guard against stereotyping the evaluation phase of the physical education lesson. This implies that the teacher should look for developments during the participation phase of the lesson that might well serve as criteria for evaluation at the end of the lesson. If the evaluation phase is always started with the question, "Did you like it?", this part of the lesson will soon become meaningless and merely time-consuming for the children. Depending upon what actually occurred during the participation phase of the lesson, the following general questions might be considered by the teacher when beginning the evaluation phase with the children.

1. Should we review briefly what we learned today?
2. What are some of the things we learned today?
3. What do we have to do or know in order to be a good performer in this game?
4. What did today's activity do for our bodies? Did it help us to have better control over our feet and legs? Did it improve our ability to throw? Did you find that you had to breathe much faster when you played this game?
5. What were some of the things you liked about the game we played today?
6. Can you think of any ways that we might improve the dance we learned today?

Questions such as these place children in a problem-solving situation and consequently provide for a more satisfactory learning situation. Moreover, this procedure is likely to provide a better setting for a child-centered physical education lesson, because children have an opportunity to discuss together ways and means for improvement in the performance of activities.

A very important feature of the evaluation phase is that the teacher has an opportunity to evaluate teaching procedures with a given group of children. In other words, the teacher should have a better understanding of how well the lesson was taught when able to hear firsthand the expressions of the children who participated.

PLANNING PHYSICAL EDUCATION LESSONS

The term *lesson plan* is the name given to a statement of achievements, together with the means by which these are to be attained as a result of the physical education activities participated in during a specified amount of time that a group spends with the teacher.

The success of any elementary school physical education program will depend to a large extent upon the daily physical education experiences of children. This implies that lessons in physical education should be carefully planned the same as in other subject areas.

Physical education lesson planning should take into account those factors that indirectly and directly influence the teaching-learning situation. This means that the teacher must consider class organization as a very important factor when daily lessons are planned, because various conditions associated with it can have an indirect influence on the physical education learning situation. For example, it will be desirable for the teacher to effect a plan of class organization that (1) is conducive to carrying out the objectives of the lesson, (2) provides sufficient activity for each child, and (3) provides for efficient and optimum use of facilities and equipment. After sufficient consideration has been given to ways and means of class organization in developing the physical education lesson, the teacher should take into account the essential characteristic features that directly influence the teaching-learning situation. In this regard, it is strongly emphasized that teachers might well devise their own lesson outlines or patterns. This procedure appears to be essential if teachers are to profit by the flexibility that is inherent in a plan that fits their own needs. With this idea in mind, the following lesson plan outline, indicating some of the features that might be incorporated into a physical education plan, is submitted as a guide for the reader.

1. *Objectives:* A statement of goals that the teacher would like to see realized during the lesson.
2. *Content:* A statement of the physical education learning activities in which the class will engage during the lesson.
3. *Class Procedures:* A brief commentary of procedures to be followed in conducting the lesson, such as (a) techniques for initiating interest and relating previous teaching-learning situations to the present lesson, (b) auditory input, (c) visual input, (d) participation, and (e) evaluation.
4. *Teaching Materials:* A statement of essential materials needed for the lesson.

If the teacher is to provide physical education learning experiences that contribute satisfactorily to total development of children, there must be a clear perspective of the total learning that is expected from the area of physical education. This implies that in order to provide for progression in physical education activities there must be some means of preserving continuity from one class period to another. Consequently, each individual lesson becomes a link in the chain of physical education learnings that contributes to the total development of the child. Experience has shown that the implementation of this theory into reality can be most successfully accomplished by wise and careful lesson planning.

Chapter Seven

PHYSICAL DEVELOPMENT OF CHILDREN THROUGH PHYSICAL EDUCATION

THERE IS AN appreciable amount of support for the idea that well-planned physical activity is a stimulant to physical growth. It is also claimed that participation in a well-balanced physical activity program is one of the ways of maintaining optimum health. Theoretically, then, a well-balanced physical education program for elementary, school-age children should be instrumental in helping them gain strength, endurance, agility, coordination, and flexibility commensurate with the energy required for a successful and happy present and future life. A program of this nature implies that every child be given the opportunity to develop to the optimum of his or her individual physical capacity in skill and ability. This is essential if each individual child is to get full benefit and optimum enjoyment from participation in physical education activities.

PHYSICAL NEEDS OF CHILDREN

If the inherent physical values mentioned above are to accrue from physical education, it becomes imperative that the program be planned on the basis of the physical needs of all children. These needs are reflected in the physical developmental characteristics of growing children. Many such characteristics are identified in the following lists of the different age levels.

This list of physical characteristics, as well as the lists of social, emotional, and intellectual characteristics, which will appear in subsequent chapters, have been developed through a documentary analysis of over a score of sources that have appeared in the

107

literature in recent years. It should be understood that these characteristics are suggestive of the behavior patterns of the so-called normal child. This implies that if a child does not conform to these characteristics, it should not be interpreted to mean that he or she is seriously deviating from the normal. In other words, it should be recognized that each child progresses at his or her own rate and that there will be much overlapping of the characteristics for each of the age levels.

Five-Year-Old Children

1. Boys' height, 42 to 46 inches; weight, 38 to 49 pounds; girls' height, 42 to 46 inches; weight, 36 to 48 pounds.
2. May grow two or three inches and gain from three to six pounds during the year.
3. Girls may be about a year ahead of boys in physiological development.
4. Beginning to have better control of body.
5. The large muscles are better developed than the small muscles that control the fingers and hands.
6. Usually determined whether he will be right– or left-handed.
7. Eye and hand coordination is not complete.
8. May have farsighted vision.
9. Vigorous and noisy, but activity appears to have definite direction.
10. Tires easily and needs plenty of rest.

Six-Year-Old Children

1. Boys height, 44 to 48 inches; weight, 41 to 54 pounds; girls' height, 43 to 48 inches; weight, 40 to 53 pounds.
2. Growth is gradual in weight and height.
3. Good supply of energy.
4. Marked activity urge absorbs him in running, jumping, chasing, and dodging games.
5. Muscular control becoming more effective with large objects.
6. There is a noticeable change in the eye-hand behavior.
7. Legs lengthening rapidly.
8. Big muscles crave activity.

Seven-Year-Old Children

1. Boys' height, 46 to 51 inches; weight, 45 to 60 pounds; girls' height, 46 to 50 inches; weight, 44 to 59 pounds.
2. Big muscle activity predominates in interest and value.
3. More improvement in eye-hand coordination.
4. May grow two or three inches and gain three to five pounds in weight during the year.
5. Tires easily and shows fatigue in the afternoon.
6. Has slow reaction time.
7. Heart and lungs are smallest in proportion to body size.
8. General health may be precarious, with susceptibility to disease high and resistance low.
9. Endurance is relatively low.
10. Coordination is improving with throwing, and catching becoming more accurate.
11. Whole-body movements are under better control.
12. Small accessory muscles developing.
13. Displays amazing amounts of vitality.

Eight-Year-Old Children

1. Boy's height, 48 to 53 inches; weight, 49 to 70 pounds; girls' height, 48 to 52 inches; weight, 47 to 66 pounds.
2. Interested in games requiring coordination of small muscles.
3. Arms are lengthening and hands are growing larger.
4. Eyes can accommodate more easily.
5. Some develop poor posture.
6. Accidents appear to occur more frequently at this age.
7. Appreciates correct skill performance.

Nine-Year-Old Children

1. Boys' height, 50 to 55 inches; weight, 55 to 74 pounds; girls' height, 50 to 54 inches; weight, 52 to 74 pounds.
2. Increasing strength in arms, hands, and fingers.
3. Endurance improving.
4. Needs and enjoys much activity; boys like to shout, wrestle, and tussle with each other.
5. A few girls near puberty.

6. Girls' gaining growth maturity up to two years over boys'.
7. Girls enjoy active group games, but are usually less noisy and less full of spontaneous energy than boys.
8. Likely to slouch and assume unusual postures.
9. Eyes are much better developed and are able to accommodate to close work with less strain.
10. May tend to overexercise.
11. Sex differences appear in recreational activities.
12. Interested in own body and wants to have questions answered.

Ten-Year-Old Children

1. Boys' height, 52 to 57 inches; weight, 59 to 82 pounds; girls' height, 52 to 57 inches; weight, 57 to 83 pounds.
2. Individuality is well-defined, and insights are more mature.
3. Stability in growth rate and stability of physiological processes.
4. Physically active and likes to rush around and be busy.
5. Before the onset of puberty there is usually a resting period or plateau, during which the boy or girl does not appear to gain in either height or weight.
6. Interested in the development of more skills.
7. Reaction time is improving.
8. Muscular strength does not seem to keep pace with growth.
9. Refining and elaborating skill in the use of small muscles.

Eleven-Year-Old Children

1. Boys' height, 53 to 58 inches; weight, 64 to 91 pounds; girls' height, 53 to 59 inches; weight, 64 to 95 pounds.
2. Marked changes in muscle system causing awkwardness and habits sometimes distressing to the child.
3. Shows fatigue more easily.
4. Some girls and a few boys suddenly show rapid growth and evidence of the approach of adolescence.
5. On the average, girls may be taller and heavier than boys.
6. Uneven growth of different parts of the body.
7. Rapid growth may result in laziness of the lateral type of child and fatigue and irritability of the linear type.
8. Willing to work hard at acquiring physical skills, and empha-

sis is on excellence of performance of physical feats.

9. Boys are more active and rough in games than girls.
10. Eye-hand coordination is well developed.
11. Bodily growth is more rapid than heart growth, and lungs are not fully developed.
12. Boys develop greater power in shoulder girdle muscles.

Twelve-Year-Old Children

1. Boys' height, 55 to 61 inches; weight, 70 to 101 pounds; girls' height, 56 to 62 inches; weight, 72 to 107 pounds.
2. Becoming more skillful in the use of small muscles.
3. May be relatively little body change in some cases.
4. Ten hours of sleep is considered average.
5. Heart rate at rest is between 80 and 90.

In those schools where a concentrated effort is being made to conduct programs to meet the physical needs of all children, there is a strong likelihood that desirable contributions are being made to physical development. On the contrary, some elementary school physical education programs as now operated cannot be justified of their contribution to physical development of all children.

EXTENT TO WHICH PHYSICAL EDUCATION CONTRIBUTES TO PHYSICAL DEVELOPMENT

Up to this point, the discussion has emphasized what physical education "should" contribute to physical development of children. However, we need to take into account the extent to which this is actually accomplished. In a recent classic report, Dr. G. Lawrence Rarick—who has been this filed's leading spokesperson on physical growth and development of children—called to attention some results of research that bears upon physical activity as it relates to physical development.[1] The following is a summary of some of the highlights of this report.

1. There is little or no evidence that planned physical activity

---

[1] L. G. Rarick, Effects of physical activity on the growth and development of children, *The Academy Papers*, no. 8, American Academy of Physical Education, Anaheim, California, March 27-28, 1974.

experiences have an influence on the growth in height of children.

2. There is sufficient information on exercise and muscle growth to provide us with general guidelines in designing physical activity programs if our purpose is to favorably affect general growth and muscular development without overdoing it.

3. One of the most striking effects of vigorous activity during the growing years is its influence upon the child's body composition, that is, the relative amount of lean, fat-free body mass. Some studies have shown that boys included in a vigorous regular physical activity program, as compared to inactive boys, substantially increased their lean body mass at the expense of fat. (The practice of excusing young obese children from physical education should perhaps be replaced by special programs of controlled diet and physical activity. This might come to pass with the implementation of Public Law 94-142, which is concerned with a program of physical education for *all* children.)

4. There is general agreement that moderate stress in the form of vigorous exercises is a positive force in building sturdy bones. However, the difficulty involved in the assessment of the exact influence of physical activity on bone growth makes it almost impossible to evaluate the effect of planned physical education programs on this aspect of growth.

5. The specific effect of school physical education programs on physical development of children shows that little or no solid data collected on a longitudinal basis exists to support the hypothesis made by many physical educators. Studies made on a short-range basis have produced varying and sometimes conflicting results. (For example, Fabricius found that fourth grade boys and girls who participated in a regular physical education program with the addition of selected calisthenics improved significantly more in physical fitness than those who participated only in the regular program.[2] On the other hand, Taddonio found no significant

---

[2]H. Fabricius, Effect of added calisthenics on the physical fitness of fourth grade boys and girls, *Research Quarterly,* May 1964.

difference between two groups of fifth grade children, one with no physical education and one with a program of fifteen-minute daily periods of calisthenics.) [3]

In summarizing research findings in this general area, Dr. Rarick suggests that while we know that the stimulus of physical activity is essential to insure the normal physical growth and physiological development of children, we do not know the amount or intensity that is necessary. In addition, its effects most assuredly vary within the individual from one period of development to another and differ widely among individuals. And, further, the importance of physical activity in the development of children goes beyond its effect on structural and morphological growth, for its true significance rests on what it does for the child as a functioning, responding being. Finally, without a sound structural organic base, unfortunate limitations are almost certain to be imposed on what might have been a strong, vigorous, and healthy child.

GUIDELINES FOR PHYSICAL DEVELOPMENT THROUGH PHYSICAL EDUCATION

It is imperative to set forth some guidelines for physical development if we are to meet with any degree of success in our attempts to provide for physical development of children through physical education. The reason for this is to assure, at least to some extent, that our efforts in attaining optimum physical development through physical education will be based upon a scientific approach. These guidelines might well take the form of valid *concepts of physical development*. This approach enables us to give serious consideration to what is known about how children grow and develop. Thus, we can select physical education experiences that are compatible with the physical developmental process. The following list of concepts of physical development are accompanied by certain implications for physical education.

1. PHYSICAL DEVELOPMENT AND CHANGE IS CONTINUOUS, ORDERLY, PROGRESSIVE, AND DIFFERENTIATED. In the early years, physical

---

[3]D. A. Taddonio, Effect of daily fifteen-minute period of calisthenics upon the physical fitness of fifth grade boys and girls, *Research Quarterly*, May 1966.

education programs might well be characterized by large muscle activities. As the child develops, more difficult types of skills and activities can be introduced so that physical education experiences progress in a way that is compatible with the child's development.

2. PHYSICAL DEVELOPMENT IS CONTROLLED BY BOTH HEREDITY AND ENVIRONMENT. The physical education program should be planned in such a way to contribute to the innate capacities of each child. Attempts should be made to establish an environmental climate where all children have an equal opportunity for wholesome participation.

3. DIFFERENCES IN PHYSICAL DEVELOPMENT OCCUR AT EACH AGE LEVEL. This implies that there should be a wide variety of activities to meet the needs of children at various developmental levels. While gearing activities to meet the needs of a particular group of children, attempts should also be made to provide for individual differences of children within the group.

4. NEEDS OF A PHYSICAL NATURE MUST BE SATISFIED IF A CHILD IS TO FUNCTION EFFECTIVELY. Physical education experiences should be planned to provide an adequate activity yield. Physical education programs should be vigorous enough to meet the physical needs of children and, at the same time, motivating enough so that they will desire to perpetuate the physical education experience outside of school.

5. VARIOUS PARTS OF THE BODY DEVELOP AT DIFFERENT RATES AND AT DIFFERENT AGES. Undue strain to the point of excessive fatigue should be avoided in physical education activities. Teachers should be aware of fatigue symptoms so that children are not likely to go beyond their physical capacity. Perhaps the use of large muscles should predominate physical education activities, at least for primary level children.

6. THE INDIVIDUAL'S OWN GROWTH PATTERN WILL VARY FROM THAT OF OTHERS BOTH AS TO TIME AND RATE. It might be well to compare a child's performance with his or her own previous achievements rather than that of classmates. It should be recognized that we should not expect the same standards of performance from all children in any given activity due to individual differences.

7. THERE ARE EARLY MATURERS AND LATE MATURERS. This concept suggests the importance of proper grouping of children within given physical education classes. The teacher should be aware as to when it will be most profitable to classify children either homogeneously or heterogeneously for certain kinds of physical education experiences.

8. THE LEVEL OF PHYSICAL MATURATION OF THE CHILD OFTEN HAS A SIGNIFICANT EFFECT ON LEARNING. Very young children should not be expected to achieve beyond their ability levels.

9. PHYSICAL DIFFERENCES MAY HAVE A MARKED EFFECT ON PERSONALITY. A variety of physical education experiences should be provided in an effort to give each child a chance to find some successful physical achievement within his or her own physical capacity. The teacher should set the example for children to learn to be respectful of physical differences by helping children to use their particular body type in the most advantageous way.

Experience has shown that when physical education programs for children are planned and implemented on the basis of what is known about how they grow and develop, there is a greater likelihood that worthwhile contributions can be made to physical development. Adherence to valid concepts of physical development is considered one of the best ways of accomplishing this goal.

EVALUATING CONTRIBUTIONS
OF PHYSICAL EDUCATION TO PHYSICAL DEVELOPMENT

Some attempt should be made to assess the potential contribution made by those physical education experiences that we provide for children. One of the first steps in this direction is to consider the physical objectives, or what we are trying to do for children physically. The broad physical objectives of physical education suggested in Chapter 3 consisted of (1) maintaining a suitable level of physical fitness, and (2) developing skill and ability.

In determining whether or not physical education experiences are contributing to the child's physical fitness, consideration needs to be given to the identification of specific components comprising the broad aspect of physical fitness. As mentioned previously, there is not complete agreement with the identification of the components of physical fitness. However, the following information provided by the President's Council on Physical Fitness and Sports[4] considers certain components to be basic as follows:

1. MUSCULAR STRENGTH. This refers to the contraction power of the muscles. The strength of muscles is usually measured by dynamometers or tensiometers, which record the amount of force particular muscle groups can apply in a single maximum effort. Man's existence and effectiveness depend upon his muscles. All movements of the body or any of its parts are impossible without action by muscles attached to the skeleton. Muscles perform vital functions of the body as well. The heart is a muscle; death occurs when it ceases to contract. Breathing, digestion, and elimination are impossible without muscular contractions. These vital muscular functions are influenced by exercising the skeletal muscles: the heart beats faster, the blood circulates through the body at a greater rate, breathing comes deep and rapid, and perspiration breaks out on the surface of the skin.

2. MUSCULAR ENDURANCE. Muscular endurance is the ability of the muscles to perform work. Two variations of muscular endurance are recognized: *isometric*, whereby a maximum static muscular contraction is held; *isotonic*, whereby the muscles continue to raise and lower a submaximal load, as in weight training or performing push-ups. In the isometric form, the muscles maintain a fixed length; in the isotonic form, they alternately shorten and lengthen. Muscular endurance must assume some muscular strength, however, there are distinctions between the two; muscle groups of the same strength may possess different degrees of endurance.

3. CIRCULATORY-RESPIRATORY ENDURANCE. Circulatory-respiratory endurance is characterized by moderate contractions of large muscle groups for relatively long periods of time during which maximal adjustments of the circulatory-respiratory system to the activity are necessary, as in distance running and swimming. Obviously, strong and enduring muscles are needed. However, by themselves, they are not enough; they do not guarantee well-developed circulatory and respiratory functions.

---

[4]*Physical Fitness Research Digest,* President's Council on Physical Fitness and Sports, Washington, D.C., series 1, no. 1, July 1971.

In addition to the basic three above, other components of physical fitness to be considered are:

1. *Muscular power:* ability to release maximum muscular force in the shortest time. Example—standing broad jump.
2. *Agility:* speed in changing direction, or body positions. Example—dodging run.
3. *Speed:* rapidity with which successive movements of the same kind can be performed. Example—50-yard dash.
4. *Flexibility:* range of movements in a joint or a sequence of joints. Example—touch fingers to floor without bending knees.
5. *Balance:* ability to maintain position and equilibrium both in movement (dynamic balance) and while stationary (static balance). Example—walking on a line or balance beam (dynamic); standing on one foot (static).
6. *Coordination:* working together of the muscles and organs of the human body in the performance of a specific task. Example—throwing or catching an object.

Having an understanding of the above components of physical fitness should be extremely helpful to the teacher in his or her efforts to evaluate the extent to which certain physical education experiences contribute to the maintenance of a suitable level of physical fitness. In fact, in planning physical education experiences for children, certain questions may be raised in connection with the activities used to bring about these experiences.

1. Does the activity provide for contraction power of muscles (muscular strength)?
2. Are there opportunities in the activity for isometric and/or isotonic muscular activity (muscular endurance)?
3. Does the activity provide for moderate contraction of large muscles for specified periods of time (circulatory-respiratory endurance)?
4. Does the activity involve ability to release maximum muscular force in a short period of time (muscular power)?
5. Is there opportunity in the activity to utilize speed in changing direction (agility)?

6. Does the activity require rapidity with successive movements of the same kind (speed) ?
7. Does the activity involve various degrees of bending at the joints (flexibility) ?
8. Is the activity one that involves the ability to maintain position and equilibrium (balance) ?
9. Is the activity concerned with the working together of the muscles and organs in specific task performance (coordination)?

Of course, it is not to be expected that all activities will involve all of the components of physical fitness. For example, while a dodgeball-type game may require various degrees of agility, it does not necessarily involve a great deal of muscular strength. However, it would be possible to select enough activities with sufficient balance of the components over a period of time so that activities as a group could contribute to the total physical fitness of the child.

It should also be clearly understood that there are limits to which we may wish to conduct activities that involve certain components of physical fitness. For instance, it is not likely that with very young children we would want to utilize too many activities involving circulatory-respiratory endurance. This, of course, presupposes that teachers will have a sufficient understanding of the growing human organism as well as an understanding of the traits and characteristics of children at the various age levels.

Not only should a teacher consider this approach in planning activities, but for purposes of value assessment after activities have been conducted. With this procedure, some judgment could be made with reference to how well a given activity attained a given purpose. It should be kept in mind that the extent to which an activity may contribute to any given component of physical fitness will likely be contingent upon a variety of factors. Included among such factors are the ability level of a given group of children; number of children in a group; general nature of the activity; difficulty in providing for individual differences; where the activity takes place; and above all, the teacher's input and behavior.

It should be obvious that any assessment made in connection

with this approach is limited because of subjectivity. Nevertheless, teachers' judgments in such matters should contain a great deal of validity, provided, as mentioned previously, that they have a clear understanding of the growing organism and the traits and characteristics at the various age levels. A rating scale for making such judgments is shown in Figure 10 and may be used as follows: The physical education activities are listed under the heading ACTIVITIES. The teacher then poses the question to himself or herself, "What is the value of this activity in terms of its contribution to the various components of physical fitness?" Using the rating scale, judgments are made accordingly. Adding the horizontal totals and dividing by nine will indicate an overall average for an activity. Adding the vertical totals and dividing by the number of activities will give the average value of each of the components of all of the activities.

The second aspect of physical development through physical education—development of skill and ability—could be evaluated in this same general manner; that is, a similar type rating scale could be used to assess the extent to which an activity requires the use of certain skills. It should be recalled that in Chapter Five these skills were classified as locomotor, axial, auxiliary, and skills of propulsion and retrieval. Figure 11 depicts a rating scale for this purpose.

PHYSICAL ACTIVITY YIELD

Another approach in determining the extent to which physical education activities contribute to physical fitness is known as *physical activity yield*. This is concerned with the amount of time that a majority of the children are meaningfully active in a physical education class period. The term *majority* can have a range of from one more than half of the children to all of the children in a class. Generally, the majority of children is considered to be 80 percent of them. This would mean that there would be activity yield for the class if twenty-four out of a class of thirty children were meaningfully active. Meaningfully active is interpreted as the children being involved in an activity, such as a game or dance, that has a specific purpose and objective.

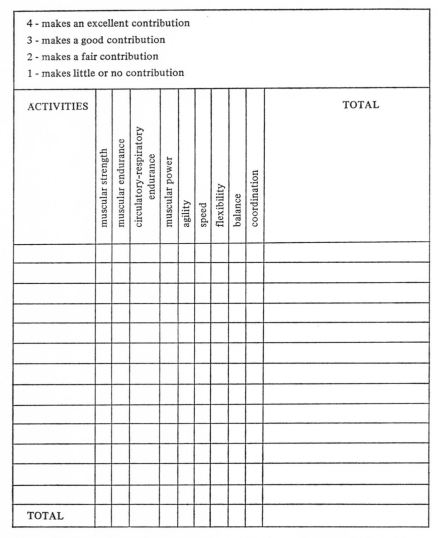

4 - makes an excellent contribution
3 - makes a good contribution
2 - makes a fair contribution
1 - makes little or no contribution

ACTIVITIES	muscular strength	muscular endurance	circulatory-respiratory endurance	muscular power	agility	speed	flexibility	balance	coordination	TOTAL
TOTAL										

Figure 10. Scale for rating potential contributions of physical education to physical fitness.

Referring back to the phases of a teaching-learning situation suggested in Chapter Six—auditory input, visual input, participation, and evaluation—it is obvious that physical activity yield

4 - provides an excellent opportunity

3 - provides a good opportunity

2 - provides a fair opportunity

1 - provides little or no opportunity

ACTIVITIES	LOCOMOTOR								AUXILIARY						PROPULSION RETRIEVAL				TOTAL
	walking	running	leaping	jumping	hopping	galloping	skipping	sliding	starting	stopping	dodging	pivoting	landing	falling	throwing	striking	kicking	catching	
TOTAL																			

Figure 11.   Scale for rating opportunities for practice of skills.

would occur only in the participation phase. Many teachers tend to agree that in a successful thirty-minute class period, eighteen to twenty minutes should be devoted to the participation phase. Some persons who have used the physical activity yield approach report a range of as low as six minutes to as high as twenty-three minutes of activity yield as defined above.

For purposes of illustration, versions of the two games, *Squirrels in Trees* and *Hill Dill* are used here to help clarify use of the idea of physical activity yield.

Squirrels in Trees

With the exception of one player, the children are arranged in groups of three. Two of the players in each group face each other and hold hands, forming a "hollow tree." The third player is a squirrel and stands between the other two in the hollow tree. The extra player—who is also a squirrel—stands near the center of the playing area. The extra player calls out "Change." On this signal, all squirrels attempt to get into a different hollow tree, and the extra squirrel also tries to find a tree. There will always be one squirrel left who does not have a tree. After playing for a time, the players are alternated so that all will have an opportunity to be a squirrel.

Hill Dill

Two parallel goal lines are established approximately sixty feet apart. One person is selected to be "it" and stands midway between the two goal lines. The rest of the group is divided into two equal groups, with one group standing on one goal line and the other on the other goal line. "It" tries to tag as many as he can while they are exchanging goals. All of those tagged become helpers, and the game continues in this manner until all but one have been tagged. This person is "it" for the next game. The game is started each time by "it" calling out, "Hill Dill run over the hill."

In Squirrels in Trees, it will be seen that at any one time only one-third of the children plus one are "meaningfully active," because the other two-thirds stand forming the hollow trees. In contrast, the game Hill Dill theoretically provides for activity yield for all of the children. This example should not be interpreted to mean that one of these activities is necessarily better than the other. It simply means that one has a greater potential for activity yield.

All physical education activities should be used to provide for certain more or less specific experiences for children. All of the various aspects of development—social, emotional, and intellectual, as well as physical—need to be taken into account in planning for physical education experiences over the long range.

It should be interesting to note that while the game Squirrels in Trees tended to provide a relatively small amount of activity yield as described above, it nevertheless is a very popular activity. Recently, I analyzed fifteen elementary school physical education books and found that this activity was recommended the greatest number of times of any game activity for first-grade children. The reader can speculate as to the reason for this. In a follow-up of a large number of elementary school physical education teachers, the same results were obtained. This could suggest that teachers to a large extent rely upon information provided in books for the kinds of activities they select for children.

The physical activity yield approach differs appreciably from the previously mentioned approach in that it is not as precise and definitive; that is, it provides only for a recognition of general physical activity engaged in by children and not for specific physical fitness components. Neither does it provide for consideration of skills used in the various activities.

In any event, the important factor to consider is that some attempt be made to arrive at an evaluation of the extent to which physical education activities contribute to the physical development of children. This, of course, requires that each physical education activity be carefully analyzed for its possible potential contribution to physical development, along with how the activity should be conducted, so that the most desirable and worthwhile results will be obtained.

Chapter Eight

SOCIAL DEVELOPMENT OF CHILDREN
THROUGH PHYSICAL EDUCATION

PHYSICAL EDUCATORS have been somewhat generous in praising their field as an outstanding medium for contributing to social development of children. This was shown in a recent analysis that I made of several elementary school physical education books. The purpose of this analysis was to identify declarative statements that proclaimed positive contributions to the various forms of development—physical, social, emotional and intellectual. Forty percent of the total number of statements indicated contributions to social development, followed by physical development with 29 percent, emotional development with 17 percent, and intellectual development with 14 percent.

While the above attests to the subjective pronouncements of the social values of physical education, at the same time it is interesting to note that little research has been conducted by physical educators to build an objective foundation under this long-held theoretical postulation. In order to examine this more thoroughly, several of my graduate students assisted me in making a documentary analysis of elementary school physical education research reported in the *Research Quarterly* over a ten-year period. This analysis yielded the following information. Seven percent of all of the studies reported met the criteria that was established to determine if a study was concerned with children of elementary school age. Seventy-seven percent of this number dealt either in whole or part with the physical aspect of personality. This compared to 19 percent with the intellectual aspect, 17 percent with the social aspect, and 10 percent with the emotional aspect. Moreover, in a very small percentage of the cases it was demonstrated that physical education made significant contributions to social development.

Most of the research that has been done in this general area has been devoted to relationships between social and physical factors. The majority of these findings generally showed that the most popular children are those who are most adept in the performance of physical skills. In this regard it is interesting to note that one study of boys and girls in grades four, five, and six revealed that both sexes expressed a preference for good school marks over excelling in sports and being popular. It was further reported that subjects selected as outstanding academically or athletically were listed as popular more often than subjects not in these categories. When outstanding students, athletes, and student-athletes (outstanding academically *and* athletically) were compared as to popularity, it was found that among boys, athletes were somewhat more popular, while among girls, student-athletes seemed to be slightly more popular.[1]

Admittedly, the whole area of sociality and physical education is difficult to study objectively, and this may be a part of the reason why so little research has been undertaken.

The above should not be interpreted to mean that physical education experiences have little to contribute to social development of children. On the contrary, the potential values of physical education in making positive contributions to social development are tremendous. One of the major functions of this chapter is to explore some of the ways in which this might be accomplished.

SOCIAL NEEDS OF CHILDREN

In a previous chapter it was mentioned that it is a relatively easy matter to identify specific components of physical fitness, but that this does not necessarily hold true for components of social fitness. Thus, in the absence of definitive components of social fitness, other directions need to be pursued in our efforts to help children achieve satisfactory levels of social fitness.

Social maturity, and hence, social fitness may be expressed in terms of fulfillment of certain social needs. In other words, if

[1]H. T. Buchanan, et al, Academic and athletic ability as popularity factors in elementary children, *Research Quarterly*, October 1976.

certain social needs are being adequately met, the child should be in a better position to realize social fitness and achieve social development. Among the general needs we should give consideration to are (1) *the need of affection,* which involves acceptance and approval of persons, (2) *the need for belonging,* which involves acceptance and approval of the group, and (3) *the need for mutuality,* which involves cooperation, mutual helpfulness, and group loyalty. The conditions for meeting these needs are inherent in many physical education experiences.

In addition to these general needs, specific needs are reflected in the developmental characteristics of growing children. Many such characteristics are identified in the following lists at the different age levels.

Five-Year-Old Children
1. Interests in neighborhood games that involve any number of children.
2. Plays various games to test his skills.
3. Enjoys other children and likes to be with them.
4. Interests are largely self-centered.
5. Seems to get along best in small groups.
6. Shows an interest in home activities.
7. Imitates when he plays.
8. Gets along well in taking turns.
9. Respects the belongings of other people.

Six-Year-Old Children
1. Self-centered and has need for praise.
2. Likes to be first.
3. Indifferent to sex distinction.
4. Enjoys group play when groups tend to be small.
5. Likes parties but behavior may not always be decorous.
6. The majority enjoy school association and have a desire to learn.
7. Interested in conduct of his friends.
8. Boys like to fight and wrestle with peers to prove masculinity.
9. Shows an interest in group approval.

Seven-Year-Old Children

1. Wants recognition for his individual achievements.
2. Sex differences are not of very great importance.
3. Not always a good loser.
4. Conversation often centers around family.
5. Learning to stand up for his own rights.
6. Interested in friends and is not influenced by their social or economic status.
7. May have nervous habits such as nail biting, tongue sucking, scratching or pulling at ear.
8. Attaining orientation in time.
9. Gets greater enjoyment from group play.
10. Shows greater signs of cooperative efforts.

Eight-Year-Old Children

1. Girls are careful of their clothes, but boys are not.
2. Leaves many things uncompleted.
3. Has special friends.
4. Has longer periods of peaceful play.
5. Does not like playing alone.
6. Enjoys dramatizing.
7. Starts collections.
8. Enjoys school and dislikes staying home.
9. Likes variety.
10. Recognition of property rights as well established.
11. Responds well to group activity.
12. Interest will focus on friends of own sex.
13. Beginning of the desire to become a member of the club.

Nine-Year-Old Children

1. Wants to be like others, talk like others, and look like them.
2. Girls are becoming more interested in their clothes.
3. Is generally a conformist and may be afraid of that which is different.
4. Able to be on his own.
5. Able to be fairly responsible and dependable.
6. Some firm and loyal friendships may develop.

7. Increasing development of qualities of leadership and followership.
8. Increasing interest in activities involving challenges and adventure.
9. Increasing participation in varied and organized group activities.

Ten-Year-Old Children

1. Begins to recognize the fallibility of adults.
2. Moving more into a peer-centered society.
3. Both boys and girls are amazingly self-dependent.
4. Self-reliance has grown and at the same time intensified group feelings are required.
5. Divergence between the two sexes is widening.
6. Great team loyalties are developing.
7. Beginning to identify with one's social contemporaries of the same sex.
8. Relatively easy to appeal to his reason.
9. On the whole, he has a fairly critical sense of justice.
10. Boys show their friendship with other boys by wrestling and jostling with each other, while girls walk around with arms around each other as friends.
11. Interest in people, in the community, and in affairs of the world is keen.
12. Interested in social problems in an elementary way and likes to take part in discussions.

Eleven-Year-Old Children

1. Internal guiding standards have been set up, and, although guided by what is done by other children, he will modify his behavior in line with those standards already set up.
2. Does a number of socially acceptable things, not because they are right *or* wrong.
3. Although obsessed by standards of peers, he is anxious for social approval of adults.
4. Need for social life companionship of children their own age.

5. Liking for organized games becoming more prominent.
6. Girls are likely to be self-conscious in the presence of boys and are usually much more mature than boys.
7. Team spirit is very strong.
8. Boys' and girls' interests are not always the same, and there may be some antagonism between the sexes.
9. Often engages in silly behavior, such as giggling and clowning.
10. Girls are more interested in social appearance than are boys.

Twelve-Year-Old Children

1. Increasing identification of self with other children of his own sex.
2. Increasing recognition of fallibility of adults.
3. May see himself as a child and adults as adults.
4. Getting ready to make the difficult transition to adolescence.
5. Pressure is being placed on individual at this level to begin to assume adult responsibilities.

It should be obvious that the above social characteristics of different age children should be taken into account if we are to meet with any degree of success in our efforts in the direction of social development through physical education.

GUIDELINES FOR SOCIAL DEVELOPMENT THROUGH PHYSICAL EDUCATION

Guidelines for social development are set forth here in the same manner that guidelines for physical development through physical education were proposed in the previous chapter; that is, these guidelines take the form of valid *concepts of social development*. When we have some basis for the social behavior of children as they grow and develop we are then in a better position to select and conduct physical education activities that are likely to be compatible with social development. The following list of concepts of social development with implications for physical education are submitted with this general idea in mind.

1. INTERPERSONAL RELATIONSHIPS ARE BASED ON SOCIAL NEEDS. All children should be given an equal opportunity in physical education participation. Moreover, the teacher should impress upon children their importance to the group. This can be done in connection with the team or group effort, which is so essential to successful participation.

2. A CHILD CAN DEVELOP HIS OR HER SELF-CONCEPT THROUGH UNDERTAKING ROLES. A child is more likely to be aware of his or her particular abilities if given the opportunity to play different positions in a team game. Rotation of such responsibilities as group leaders tends to provide opportunity for self-expression of children through role playing.

3. THERE ARE VARIOUS DEGREES OF INTERACTION BETWEEN INDIVIDUALS AND GROUPS. The physical education experience should provide for an outstanding setting for the child to develop interpersonal interaction. The teacher has the opportunity to observe children in movement situations rather than in only sedentary situations. Consequently, the teacher is in a good position to guide integrative experiences by helping children to see the importance of satisfactory interrelationships in a physical education group situation.

4. CHOOSING AND BEING CHOSEN—AN EXPRESSION OF A BASIC NEED—IS A FOUNDATION OF INTERPERSONAL RELATIONSHIPS. As often as possible, children should be given the opportunity for choosing teammates, partners, and the like. However, great caution should be taken by the teacher to see that this is carried out in an equitable way. The teacher should devise ways of choice so that certain children are not always selected last or left out entirely.

5. LANGUAGE IS A BASIC MEANS AND ESSENTIAL ACCOMPANIMENT OF SOCIALIZATION. Children can be taught the language of the body through using the names of its parts as they participate in physical education. This is an important dimension in the development of body awareness. Physical education experiences should be such that there is opportunity for oral expression among and between children. For example, in the evaluation phase of a physical education lesson, children have a fine opportunity for meaningful oral expression if the evaluation is skillfully guided by the teacher.

6. LEARNING TO PLAY ROLES IS A PROCESS OF SOCIAL DEVELOPMENT. A child should be given the opportunity to play as many roles as possible in the physical education experience. This could include being involved in the organization and administration of physical education activities such as selection of activities, making rules of play, and helping others with skills. Doing a physical skill is in itself the playing of a role, such as being a better rope jumper, dancer, and the like. Thus, the very medium of physical education activity is the process of social adjustment.

7. INTEGRATIVE INTERACTION TENDS TO PROMOTE SOCIAL DEVELOPMENT. The key word in this process to promote development is *action*, which is the basis for physical education. Physical education is unique in its potential to accomplish integrative interaction, and thus promote social development. Spontaneity can be considered as one of the desired outcomes of integrative experiences, which means the opportunity for actions and feelings expressed by the child as he or she really is. Active play is perhaps the most important aspect of life for young children, and, thus, spontaneous actions and feelings are best expressed through activity.

8. RESISTANCE TO DOMINATION IS AN ACTIVE ATTEMPT TO MAINTAIN ONE'S INTEGRITY. The teacher might well consider child resistance as a possible indicator of teacher domination. If this occurs, the teacher might look into his or her actions, which may be dominating the teaching-learning situation. Child resistance should be interpreted as a sign of a healthful personality, and a wise teacher will likely be able to direct the energy into constructive channels to promote social development. A very natural outlet for this frustrated energy is found in desirable activities presented in the physical education program.

9. INTERPERSONAL INTERACTION BETWEEN CHILDREN IS A BASIS FOR CHOICE. If children are left out by other children, this symptom should be studied with care to see if this is an indication of poor interpersonal relationships with other children. Very interesting aspects of interpersonal relationships can be observed by the wise teacher. Children may realize the value of a child to a specific activity and accept such a child accordingly. On the other hand, they may be likely to accept their friends regardless of

ability in physical education skills.

10. A CHILD, IN AND AS A RESULT OF BELONGING TO A GROUP, DEVELOPS DIFFERENTLY THAN HE OR SHE CAN AS AN INDIVIDUAL ALONE.   Most physical education activities provide for an outstanding opportunity for children to engage actively in a variety of group experiences.   Merely being a member of a group can be a most rewarding experience for a child.   If properly conducted, physical education group activities should provide an optimal situation for desirable social development because children focus their greatest personal interest in active play.

SOME POSSIBILITIES FOR SOCIAL DEVELOPMENT THROUGH PHYSICAL EDUCATION

It has already been suggested that the physical education "laboratory" should present near-ideal surroundings and environment for the social development of children.   It has also been indicated that physical educators are convinced that this area of the school curriculum provides some of the best means for teaching vital social skills.   The following generalized discussion is intended to elaborate some of these possibilities.

There are numerous physical education situations through which children may gain a better understanding of the importance of cooperation.   By their very nature, many games depend upon the cooperation of group members in achieving a common goal. Dancing is an activity that requires persons to perform together in a synchronization of rhythmic patterns.   In skills such as throwing and catching there must be a coordinated action of the thrower and catcher.   In certain kinds of gymnastic activities, children participate and learn together in groups of three—two children assisting the performer and the others taking turns in performing. In these and countless other situations the importance of cooperating together for the benefit of the individual and the group is readily discerned.

It has been demonstrated in numerous occasions that children can gain insight into the way of life of our own people and people of other lands by learning dances and games engaged in by these people.   In that active play is perhaps the one best medium for child understanding, this procedure is a particularly noteworthy one. Early American country dances and nationality dances, as well as various kinds of period games and games from foreign lands, provide children with an opportunity to see the significance between the activities and the cultural and physical aspects that bear upon them.

Leadership and followership activities may be engaged in games such as *Follow the Leader*, with one child selected to be the leader and others following and attempting to do the same things.

Group consciousness and friendliness within a group can be developed in certain physical education activities. For example, some teachers feel that games played from a circle formation have a positive psychological effect in that they tend to provide a spirit of unity among the participants; that is, each player can see and become aware of the performance of other players in the group. It is interesting to note that holding hands in a circle game has important connotations for social interaction through *tactile communication*. Some writers have called attention to the possibilities of this by suggesting that better human relations can be obtained through intrinsic tactile communication in the utilization of activities requiring *touch*.[2] In fact, a recent study substantiates the idea that such tactile communication provides a basis for the attraction that is necessary for black and white children to form positive relationships. More specifically, this study found that recorded incidents of tactile interaction between black and white children were equivalent to the recorded incidents of tactile interaction between black children and black children and those between white children and white children.[3]

In spite of such findings, circle games have been much maligned on the basis that there is too much inactivity of children just standing in a circle. It is doubtful if such criticism is entirely justified, because the skillful teacher can conduct this type of activity in such a way that there will be equal opportunity for participation.

---

[2] S. B. Johnson, and D. A. Pease, Tactile communication in sport, *Journal of Health, Physical Education and Recreation*, February 1974.

[3] S. B. Johnson, The effects of tactile communication in sport on changes in interpersonal relationships between black and white children, Master's Thesis, Memphis State University, Memphis, Tennessee, 1973.

The natural opportunities for wholesome group experiences in games provide a means for the development of ability to get along with various kinds of people. One teacher, confronted with the problem of getting a fourth-grade class to be more congenial employed the game called *Hook On.* In a version of this game, one player is selected to be "it" and another is selected to be the chaser. These two take positions at opposite ends of the activity area. The other players form couples by linking arms with a partner, and the couples take places anywhere in the playing area. At a signal, the chaser attempts to tag "it," who dodges in and out between the couples. In order to avoid being tagged, "it" can "hook on" to a free arm of one of the couples. At this time, the other person of that couple becomes "it," and the game proceeds in this manner. The teacher found that this particular activity helped to eliminate certain cliques that were being formed in the class. She noticed that children did not always hook on to their friends, since out of necessity they needed to hook on to any available couple to avoid being tagged.

Issues that might come up as a result of certain misunderstandings in physical education activities give rise to the exercise of wholesome social controls. The relationships of these controls in physical education experiences to those in community living might possibly be understood in varying degrees by children at the different age levels. In these situations, outstanding settings are provided for the development of problem-solving techniques in which children are placed to make value judgments.

Some physical education teachers have observed that while physical education provides opportunities to encourage interpersonal communication and understanding among children, at the same time these opportunities are occasionally manifested in the form of minor conflict situations. A procedure used to help solve such minor conflicts has been suggested by Robert Horrocks. He refers to it as the "talking bench" where two children sit until they have agreed upon the origin of their conflict and resolved it to the satisfaction of both.[4]

The fact that children of elementary school age are capable of

[4] R. N. Horrocks, Resolving conflicts in the gymnasium, *Journal of Physical Education and Recreation,* September 1978.

decision making in physical education situations is shown in a recent study. The purpose of this study was to determine the difference between two decision-making models on the attitudes and interaction patterns of elementary school children in human movement. Children from grades one through six participated in either a program where the teacher made all the decisions or in a program where they shared in decision making. The results indicated more positive attitudes for children involved in decision making as well as more positive attitudes for the younger children. Children given the opportunity to share in decision making showed greater interaction with the teachers and greater initiative and contributions.[5]

The above discussions included but a few of the numerous possibilities for social control, social interaction, and thus social development, which are likely to be inherent in the physical education experience. Admittedly, this does not accrue automatically, and any degree of success in social development through physical education rests heavily upon the teacher.

INTEGRATING PHYSICAL EDUCATION AND SOCIAL STUDIES

A practice that I have found quite useful is that of integrating physical education and social studies. A possible reason for this is that some of the objectives of the social studies program in the elementary school are highly compatible with the social objectives of physical education. Some of the objectives of the social studies program include (1) to help children live by democratic processes; (2) to help children learn the procedures involved in problem solving; and (3) to help children develop appreciation of leadership and followership. Potential opportunities for acquiring these knowledges and appreciations are abundant in practically all phases of the elementary school physical education program.

The idea that desirable social studies experiences can be provided through physical education has been endorsed over the years by various educators. For example, a good many years ago, Cramer

---

[5]V. H. Mancini, T. F. Cheffers, and L. D. Zaichkowsky, Decision making in elementary children: effects on attitudes, and interactions, *Research Quarterly*, March 1976.

and Domian stated that, "Naturally, the activities in physical education cannot be separated from the other activities and subjects in any classroom. They contribute to the total program; to learning in social studies through games and folk dances of other people in other lands. . . ."[6]

Physical Education in Social Studies Units

When the history of education is considered over a period of several hundred years, the "unit" may be thought of as a more or less recent innovation. Because of this it is difficult to devise a universal definition for the term *unit*. This is partly due to the fact that the term does not at the present time have a fixed meaning in the field of education. Essentially, the purpose of unitary teaching is to provide for a union of component related parts that evolve into a systematic totality. In other words, the unit should consist of a number of interrelated learnings that are concerned with a specific topic or central theme. A variety of types of experiences as well as various curriculum areas are drawn upon for the purpose of enriching the learning medium for all children so that the understandings of the topic in question can be developed.

It will not be the purpose here to consider the advantages or disadvantages of the various types of units that have been discussed in textbooks and the periodical literature. On the contrary, it will be the purpose of this section of the chapter to discuss the role of physical education as a curriculum area to be "drawn upon for the purpose of enriching the learning medium for all children so that the understandings of the topic in question can be developed."

There is universal agreement among educators that the things children do—the activities—are by far the most important part of the unit. Yet, those experiences through which children may be likely to learn best, that is, active play experiences, have been grossly neglected as essential and important activities of the unit. There is, however, an explanation for this paradoxical phenomenon. For example, the classroom teacher, who is in most cases well prepared to guide and direct many learning activities and

---

[6]R. V. Cramer, and Domian, O. E., *Administration and Supervision in the Elementary School*, New York, Harper, 1960, p. 234-235.

experiences of the unit, may not feel confident enough to include physical education activities as a means of developing the concepts of the unit. Moreover, when there is a physical education specialist available to assist the classroom teacher, this individual may not feel familiar enough with the social studies curriculum to recommend physical education activities that will be of value in developing unit concepts. However, some elementary school physical educators are doing outstanding work in helping classroom teachers in the integration of physical education and social studies. For instance, some elementary school curriculum guides devote a section to activities related to social studies. Practices of this kind are to be commended but at the same time they may take place in far too few cases. An examination of large numbers of social studies units has indicated this to be true and perhaps for the reasons mentioned.

The reader should not interpret the previous discussion to mean that the recommendation of the use of physical education activities as learning activities of social studies is something new. In fact, on occasion, this procedure has been recommended by persons outside the field of physical education. Almost half a century ago, Lois Mossman developed a list of the things that people do. These activities were classified into ten groups with a total of eighty different activities. It is interesting to note that some of the activities were concerned exactly with the "things that children do" in physical education, such as *playing, dancing,* and *recreating.*[7]

In order to show more clearly how physical education activities can be used as a means of extending the basis for learning in social studies units, a concrete example is submitted at this point. This example is concerned with the use of a game activity in introducing a third grade social studies unit on "Helping Others." The game used for this purpose was *Hill Dill*, which was described in Chapter 7. It should be recalled that all players tagged became helpers. The teacher had the children play the game and then evaluated it with them, guiding the discussion about the importance of helping. This discussion developed into

---

[7]L. C. Mossman, *The Activity Concept,* New York, Macmillan, 1938, p. 54.

a teacher-pupil planning session, and the unit on *Helping Others* began with a high level of interest.

Obviously, this procedure requires close cooperation between the classroom teacher and the physical education teacher, and it also requires creative thinking on the parts of both. When these individuals work together in this manner they should be able to develop physical education learning activities that will be of value in integrating physical education and social studies.

IMPLICATIONS OF RESEARCH
IN SOCIAL BEHAVIOR OF CHILDREN

As has been mentioned previously, not a great deal of research has been undertaken in the field of physical education in relation to social development of children. This being the case, we should consider the psychological research that has been conducted in social development so that we can draw some implications for physical education. This is to say that in utilizing such findings, we will be better able to conduct physical education experiences that are more likely to result in positive social development. A recent report by the National Institute of Education provides some information that might be useful.[8]

The purpose of the report was to provide preschool and early elementary school teachers with a summary of current psychological research concerned with the social development of young children. In submitting the report, the authors noted that caution should prevail with reference to basic research and practical implications. In this regard, the following suggestions are submitted.

1. What seems "true" at one point in time often becomes "false" when new information becomes available or when new theories change the interpretation of old findings.
2. Substantial problems arise in any attempt to formulate practical suggestions for professionals in one discipline based on research findings from another discipline.
3. Throughout the report, recommendations for teachers have

---

[8]W. Roedell, R. G. Slaby, and H. B. Robinson, Social development in young children, a report for teachers, Washington, D.C., National Institute of Education, U.S. Department of Health, Eduaction and Welfare, January 1976.

been derived from logical extensions of experimental findings and classroom adaptations of experimental procedures.

4. Some of the proposed procedures may prove unworkable in the classroom, even though they may make sense from a psychological perspective.

5. When evaluating potential applications of psychological findings it is important to remember that psychological research is usually designed to derive probability statements about the behavior of groups of people.

6. Individual teachers may work better with a procedure that is, on the average, less effective.

The following list of generalizations, which have been derived from the findings, are accompanied by possible general implications for physical education. In considering these implications, the above cautions should be kept in mind. Moreover, each individual teacher will no doubt be able to draw his or her own implications and make practical applications that apply to particular situations.

1. REASONING WITH AN EMPHASIS ON CONSEQUENCES FOR OTHER PEOPLE IS ASSOCIATED WITH THE DEVELOPMENT OF A HUMANISTIC CONCERN FOR OTHERS. Teachers might consider encouragement of social behavior in the physical education experience by discussing the implications of children's and teachers' actions for the feelings of others; poor performers should be encouraged rather than ridiculed.

2. CHILDREN TEND TO SHOW EMPATHY TOWARD INDIVIDUALS SIMILAR TO THEMSELVES. In the physical education experience it is important to emphasize the likenesses of people; while all children may differ in one or more characteristics, they still are more alike than they are different.

3. CHILDREN MAY LEARN TECHNIQUES FOR POSITIVE SOCIAL INTERACTION BY OBSERVING CHILDREN WHO ARE BEHAVING COOPERATIVELY. In game activities particularly, cooperation of each individual is very important to the success of the group; the teacher can suggest ways children can cooperate and reinforce children when these suggestions are followed.

4. THE MORE FREQUENTLY CHILDREN VOLUNTARILY PRACTICE

SOCIAL SKILLS, THE MORE LIKELY THEY ARE TO USE THESE SKILLS IN LESS STRUCTURED SITUATIONS. In the physical education situation, children can be assigned certain responsibilities that require the practice of social skills. The physical education teacher can co-ordinate this experience with the classroom teacher, and each can determine the results of the other's efforts.

5. CHILDREN ARE LIKELY TO USE BEHAVIORS FOR WHICH THEY HAVE BEEN REINFORCED. The teacher can focus his or her attention on children who are cooperating, sharing, and helping the teacher and other children in the physical education situation.

6. CHILDREN ARE LIKELY TO IMITATE BEHAVIORS FOR WHICH THEY SEE OTHER CHILDREN BEING REINFORCED. The teacher can compliment those children who are saying cooperative, helpful things to each other, particularly in participation in game activi-ties. At the same time, the teacher should consider simultaneously ignoring negative social interactions of children.

7. CHILDREN ARE LIKELY TO HELP AND SHARE WHEN THEY HAVE SEEN SOMEONE ELSE DO IT, PARTICULARLY IF THEY KNOW AND LIKE THE MODEL. The physical education teacher can take the lead by providing examples of sharing, helping, and cooperating.

8. IGNORED BEHAVIOR MAY INCREASE AT FIRST, BUT EVENTUALLY IT IS LIKELY TO DECREASE IF THE CHILD DOES NOT RECEIVE REIN-FORCEMENT FROM OTHER SOURCES. The teacher may wish to pointedly ignore misbehavior whenever possible by turning away from the misbehaving child and attending to a child who is be-having appropriately. Obviously, all misbehavior cannot be ignored because in some instances such misbehavior might be concerned with safety factors in the physical education experience. Thus, it is sometimes appropriate for the teacher to act expedi-ently.

9. CONSISTENT, IMMEDIATE PUNISHMENT MAY TEND TO DISCOUR-AGE THE BEHAVIOR IT FOLLOWS. When this is necessary, the teach-er might consider choosing mild punishment related to the activ-ity, which can follow misbehavior immediately. For example, if a child is misusing a piece of material such as a ball, it can be re-moved, at least temporarily.

10. REASONING CAN INCREASE CHILDREN'S AWARENESS OF THE NEEDS OF OTHERS, AND IT (REASONING) IS A FORM OF ATTENTION THAT

SHOULD BE LIMITED TO OCCASIONS WHEN CHILDREN ARE BEHAVING APPROPRIATELY. In many teaching-learning situations in physical education there is a need for certain rules and regulations. It might be well to discuss the reasoning behind rules when children are following the rules and *not* when the rules are disobeyed. However, this does not necessarily preclude a negative approach if a given situation warrants it.

In closing this discussion, it should be reiterated that each individual reader will no doubt be able to draw his or her own implications and make practical applications that apply to particular physical education situations.

EVALUATING CONTRIBUTIONS OF PHYSICAL EDUCATION TO SOCIAL DEVELOPMENT

It has already been mentioned that physical educators place great store in the contributions of their field to social development of children. It has also been suggested that little solid scientific evidence is available to support this belief. This makes it all the more important that physical education teachers examine as critically as possible those physical education experiences that are being provided for children.

Processes for Evaluating Social Growth in Physical Education

In the past, most of what has been done in this area has been of a subjective nature. The process of "observation" has been considered satisfactory because it has been felt that for the most part we can merely watch children to see the kinds of relationships that exist between them.

In more recent years, some teachers have approached this problem from a more scientific standpoint and have used certain *sociometric techniques* with varying degrees of success. Included among such techniques are (1) sociograms, (2) sociographs, and (3) social distance scales.

Sociograms

In this technique, a child is usually asked to name in order of preference those persons liked best in a group. In the physical education situation, a child may be asked to name those he or she would like to be with or play with most. After the choices are made, the results are plotted on a sociogram.

If two children choose each other, they are known as "mutual choices of pairs." Those not selected by anyone in the group and who do not choose anyone are called "isolates." "Islands" is the name given to pairs or small groups of mutual choices not selected by any in the large group. While the sociogram is a worthwhile device for identifying certain aspects of interpersonal relationships, it is a time-consuming procedure and for this reason is not one of the more popular methods used by physical education teachers.

Sociographs

The sociograph is a more expedient and practical way of tabulating and interpreting data. Instead of plotting as in a sociogram, choices are recorded in tabular form opposite the names of children. This readily shows the number of rejections, mutual choices, choices received, and choices given.

Social Distance Scales

This sociometric technique has been used in research in social psychology for over fifty years. In this procedure, each member of a group is asked to check the other members according to certain degrees of social intimacy such as:

1. Would like to have him as one of my best friends.
2. Would like to have him in my group, but not as a close friend.
3. Would like to be with him once in a while, but not often or for very long.
4. Do not mind his being in the group, but I do not want anything to do with him.
5. Wish he were not in the group.

This procedure can be used as a physical education class social distance scale to attempt to determine the general social tone of a class. Class social distance scores on each individual child can be obtained by arbitrarily weighting the items listed above. For example, if a child was checked two times for item number one

$(2 \times 1 = 2)$; six times for item two $(6 \times 2 = 12)$; eight times for item three $(8 \times 3 = 24)$; three times for item four $(3 \times 4 = 12)$; and one time for item five $(1 \times 5 = 5)$ the total score would be 55. (The lower the score the greater the acceptance by the group and the less the social distance.)

These data can be used to determine, with some degree of objectivity, the extent to which physical education has contributed to social relationships, that is, a teacher can compare scores before and after a group of children have been involved in a particular physical education experience.

Over a period of years, I have used all of the above sociometric techniques with varying degrees of success. In some instances, the results have provided guidance in efforts to obtain a better understanding of social relationships and thus contribute to social development. It is recognized that all teachers are aware of those obvious factors concerned with group social structure. However, the many aspects of interpersonal relationships that are not so obvious can be difficult to discern. It is the purpose of sociometric techniques to assist in the emergence of these relationships.

Chapter Nine

EMOTIONAL DEVELOPMENT
OF CHILDREN
THROUGH PHYSICAL EDUCATION

IN A PREVIOUS discussion of emotion it was suggested that the emotional objective of physical education should imply that sympathetic guidance should be provided in meeting anxieties, joys, and sorrows and help given in developing aspirations and security. In order to attempt to reach this objective, we might well consider emotions from a standpoint of the growing child in terms of maturing emotionally.

For purposes of this discussion, I will consider maturity as being concerned with a state of readiness on the part of the organism. The term is most frequently used in connection with age relationships. For example, it may be said that "Johnny is mature for six years of age." Simply stated, emotional maturity is the process of acting one's age.

Generally speaking, emotional maturity will be achieved through a gradual accumulation of mild and pleasant emotions. On the contrary, emotional immaturity indicates that unpleasant emotions have accumulated too rapidly for the individual to absorb. In order for us to pursue a sensible course in helping the child become more emotionally mature, there are certain factors concerned with emotional development that need to be taken into account. Some of these factors are the subject of the ensuing discussion.

FACTORS CONCERNING EMOTIONAL DEVELOPMENT

Some of the factors concerned with emotional development that need to be considered are (1) characteristics of childhood emotionality, (2) emotional arousals and reactions, and (3) factors that influence emotionality.

Characteristics of Childhood Emotionality

1. ORDINARILY, THE EMOTIONS OF CHILDREN ARE NOT LONG LASTING. A child's emotions may last for a few minutes or less and then terminate rather abruptly. The child gets it "out of his or her system" so to speak by expressing it outwardly. In contrast, some adult emotions may be long and drawn out. As children get older, expressing the emotions by overt action is encumbered by certain social restraints. This is to say that what might be socially acceptable at one age level is not necessarily so at another. This may be a reason for some children developing moods, which in a sense are states of emotion drawn out over a period of time and expressed slowly. Typical moods of childhood may be that of "sulking" due to restraint of anger, being "jumpy" from repressed fear, and becoming "humorous" from controlled joy or happiness.

2. THE EMOTIONS OF CHILDREN ARE LIKELY TO BE INTENSE. This might be confusing to some adults who do not understand child behavior, that is, they may not be able to see why a child would react rather violently to a situation that to them might appear insignificant.

3. THE EMOTIONS OF CHILDREN ARE SUBJECT TO RAPID CHANGE. A child is capable of shifting rapidly from laughing to crying, or from anger to joy. Although the reason for this is not definitely known, it might be that there is not as much depth of feeling among children as there is among adults. In addition, it could be due to the lack of experience that children have had as well as their stage of intellectual development. We do know that young children have a short attention-span, which could cause them to change rapidly from one kind of emotion to another.

4. THE EMOTIONS OF CHILDREN CAN APPEAR WITH A HIGH DEGREE OF FREQUENCY. As children get older, they manage to develop the ability to adjust to situations that previously would have

caused an emotional reaction. This is probably due to the child's acquiring more experience with various kinds of emotional situations. Perhaps a child learns through experience what is socially acceptable and what is socially unacceptable. This is particularly true if the child is reprimanded in some way following a violent emotional reaction. For this reason, the child may try to confront situations in ways that do not involve an emotional response.

5. CHILDREN DIFFER IN THEIR EMOTIONAL RESPONSES. One child confronted with a situation that instills fear may run away from the immediate environment. Another may hide behind his mother. Still another might just stand there and cry. Different reactions of children to emotional situations are probably due to a host of factors. Included among these may be past experience with a certain kind of emotional situation; willingness of parents and other adults to help children become independent; and family relationships in general.

6. STRENGTH OF CHILDREN'S EMOTIONS ARE SUBJECT TO CHANGE. At some age levels certain kinds of emotions may be weak and later become stronger. Conversely, with some children, emotions that were strong may tend to decline. For example, small children may be timid among strangers, but later when they see there is nothing to fear, the timidity is likely to wane.

Emotional Arousals and Reactions

If we are to understand the emotions of children, we need to take into account those factors of emotional arousal and how children might be expected to react to them. Many different kinds of emotional patterns have been identified. For purposes here, I have arbitrarily selected for discussion the emotional states of fear, worry, anger, jealousy, and joy.

1. FEAR. It is possible that it is not necessarily the arousal itself, but rather the way something is presented that determines whether there will be a fear reaction. For example, in a physical education class if there is a discussion of a certain gymnastic activity in terms of "If you do it this way you will break your neck," it is possible a fear response will occur. This is one of the many reasons for using a positive approach in teaching, especially in the area of physical education.

A child may react to fear by withdrawing. With very young children this may be in the form of crying or breath holding. With a child under three, and in some older children as well, the "ostrich" approach may be used, that is, he may hide his face in order to get away from it. As children get older, these forms of reaction may decrease or cease altogether because of social pressures. For instance, it may be considered "sissy" to cry, especially among boys.   (The validity of this kind of thinking is of course open to question.)

2. WORRY. This might be considered an imaginary form of fear, and it can be a fear not aroused directly from the child's environment. Worry can be aroused by imagining a situation that could possibly arise, that is; a child could worry about not being able to perform well in a certain physical education situation. Since worries are likely to be caused by imaginary rather than real conditions, they are not likely to be found in abundance among very young children. Perhaps the reason for this is that they have not reached a stage of intellectual development where they might imagine certain things that would cause worry. While children will respond to worry in different ways, certain manifestations such as nail biting may be symptomatic of this condition.

3. ANGER. This emotional response tends to occur more frequently than that of fear. This is probably due to the fact that there are more conditions that incite anger. In addition, some children quickly learn that anger may get attention that otherwise would not be forthcoming. It is likely that as children get older they may show more anger responses than fear responses because they soon see that there is not too much to fear.

Anger is caused by many factors, one of which is interference with movements the child wants to execute. This interference can come from others or by the child's own limitations in ability and physical development. This, of course, can be an important factor in the performance of certain tasks in physical education.

Because of individual differences in children, there is a wide variation in anger responses. In general, these responses are either *impulsive* or *inhibited*. In impulsive responses, the child manifests an overt action either toward another person or an object that caused the anger. For instance, a child who collides with a door might take out the anger by hitting or kicking the door. (This form of child behavior is also sometimes manifested by some "adults.") Inhibited responses are likely to be kept under control, and as children mature emotionally they acquire more ability to control their anger.

4. JEALOUSY. This response usually occurs when a child feels a threat of loss of affection. Many psychologists believe that jealousy is closely related to anger. Because of this the child may build up resentment against another person. Jealousy can be very devastating in childhood, and every effort should be made to avoid it.

Jealousy is concerned with social interaction that involves persons the child likes. These individuals can be parents, siblings, teachers, and peers. There are various ways in which the child may respond. These include (1) being aggressive toward the one he is jealous of, or possibly toward others as well, (2) withdrawing from the person whose affections he thinks have been lost, and (3) possible development of an "I don't care" attitude.

In some cases children will not respond in any of the above ways. They might try to excel over the person of whom they are jealous. In other words, they may tend to do things to impress the person whose affections they thought have been lost.

5. JOY. This pleasant emotion is one that we strive for because it is so important in maintaining emotional stability. Causes of joy differ from one age level to another and from one child to another at the same age level. This is to say that what might be a joyful situation for one person may not necessarily be so for another.

Joy is expressed in various ways, but the most common are laughing and smiling, the latter being a restrained form of laughter. Some people respond to joy with a state of body relaxation. This is difficult to detect because it has little or no overt manifestation. However, it may be noticed when one compares it with body tension caused by unpleasant emotions.

EMOTIONAL NEEDS OF CHILDREN

It has already been mentioned in a previous chapter that it was a relatively easy matter to identify specific components of physical fitness. This did not hold true for social fitness, and neither does it hold true for emotional fitness. Therefore, in the absence of definitive components of emotional fitness, we need to look in other directions in our efforts to help children maintain satisfactory levels of emotional fitness.

Emotional maturity, and, hence, emotional fitness could be expressed in terms of the fulfillment of certain emotional needs. These needs can be reflected in the developmental characteristics of growing children. A number of emotional characteristics are identified in the following lists at the different age levels.

Five-Year-Old Children

1. Seldom shows jealousy toward younger siblings.
2. Usually sees only one way to do a thing.
3. Usually sees only one answer to a question.
4. Inclined not to change plans in the middle of an activtiy, but would rather begin over.
5. May fear being deprived of mother.
6. Some definite personality traits evidenced.
7. Is learning to get along better, but still may resort to quarreling and fighting.
8. Likes to be trusted with errands.
9. Enjoys performing simple tasks.
10. Wants to please and do what is expected of him.
11. Is beginning to sense right and wrong in terms of specific situations.

Six-Year-Old Children

1. Restless and may have difficulty in making decisions.
2. Emotional pattern of anger may be difficult to control at times.
3. Behavior patterns may often be explosive and unpredictable.

4. Jealousy toward siblings at times; at other times takes pride in siblings.
5. Greatly excited by anything new.
6. Behavior susceptible to shifts in direction, inwardly motivated and outwardly stimulated.
7. May be self-assertive and dramatic.

Seven-Year-Old Children

1. Curiosity and creative desires may condition responses.
2. May be difficult to take criticism from adults.
3. Wants to be more independent.
4. Reaching for new experiences and trying to relate himself to enlarged world.
5. Overanxious to reach goals set by parents and teachers.
6. Critical of himself and sensitive to failure.
7. Emotional pattern of anger is more controlled.
8. Becoming less impulsive and boisterous in actions than at six.

Eight-Year-Old Children

1. Dislikes taking much criticism from adults.
2. Can give and take criticism in his own group.
3. May develop enemies.
4. Does not like to be treated as a child.
5. Has a marked sense of humor.
6. First impulse is to blame others.
7. Becoming more realistic and wants to find out for himself.

Nine-Year-Old Children

1. May sometimes be outspoken and critical of the adults he knows, although he has a genuine fondness for them.
2. Responds best to adults who treat him as an individual and approach him in an adult way.
3. Likes recognition for what he has done and responds well to deserved praise.
4. Likely to be backward about public recognition, but likes private praise.

5. Developing sympathy and loyalty to others.
6. Does not mind criticism or punishment if he thinks it is fair, but is indignant if he thinks it is unfair.
7. Disdainful of danger to and safety of himself, which may be a result of increasing interest in activities involving challenges and adventure.

Ten-Year-Old Children

1. Increasing tendency to rebel against adult domination.
2. Capable of loyalties and hero worship, and he can inspire it in his schoolmates.
3. Can be readily inspired to group loyalties in his club organization.
4. Likes the sense of solidarity that comes from keeping a group secret as a member of a group.
5. Each sex has an increasing tendency to show lack of sympathy and understanding with the other.
6. Boys' and girls' behavior and interests becoming increasingly different.

Eleven-Year-Old Children

1. If unskilled in group games and game skills, he may tend to withdraw.
2. Boys may be concerned if they feel they are underdeveloped.
3. May appear to be indifferent and uncooperative.
4. Moods change quickly.
5. Wants to grow up, but may be afraid to leave childhood security behind.
6. Increase in self-direction and in a serious attitude toward work.
7. Need for approval to feel secure.
8. Beginning to have a fully developed idea of own importance.

Twelve-Year-Old Children

1. Beginning to develop a truer picture of morality.
2. Clearer understanding of real causal relations.

3. The process of sexual maturation involves structural and physiological changes with possible perplexing and disturbing emotional problems.

4. Personal appearance may become a source of great conflict, and learning to appreciate good grooming or the reverse may be prevalent.

5. May be very easily hurt when criticized or made the scapegoat.

6. Maladjustments may occur when there is not a harmonious relationship between child and adults.

It should be obvious that the above emotional characteristics reflect some of the emotional needs of children at the different age levels. These characteristics should be taken into account in the physical education teaching-learning situation if we expect to meet with success these needs of children.

GUIDELINES FOR EMOTIONAL DEVELOPMENT THROUGH PHYSICAL EDUCATION

Guidelines for emotional development are set forth here in the same manner that guidelines for physical and social development through physical education were proposed in the two previous chapters; that is, these guidelines take the form of valid "concepts of emotional development." When we have a basis for the emotional behavior of children as they grow and develop, we are then in a better position to provide physical education experiences that are likely to be compatible with emotional development. The following list of concepts of emotional development with implications for physical education are submitted with this general idea in mind.

1. AN EMOTIONAL RESPONSE MAY BE BROUGHT ABOUT BY A GOAL'S BEING FURTHERED OR THWARTED. The teacher should make a very serious effort to assure successful physical education experiences for every child. This can be accomplished in part by attempting to provide for individual differences within given physical education experiences. The physical education setting should be such that each child derives a feeling of personal worth through making some sort of positive contribution.

2. SELF-REALIZATION EXPERIENCES SHOULD BE CONSTRUCTIVE. The opportunity for creative experience inherent in physical education affords the child an excellent chance for self-realization through physical expression. Teachers might consider planning with children themselves to see that activities are meeting their needs and, as a result, involve a constructive experience.

3. EMOTIONAL RESPONSES INCREASE AS THE DEVELOPMENT OF THE CHILD BRINGS GREATER AWARENESS, THE ABILITY TO REMEMBER THE PAST AND TO ANTICIPATE THE FUTURE. The teacher can remind the children of their past emotional responses with words of praise. This should encourage children to repeat such responses in future similar physical education situations and, thus, make for a better learning situation.

4. AS THE CHILD DEVELOPS, THE EMOTIONAL REACTIONS TEND TO BECOME LESS VIOLENT AND MORE DISCRIMINATING. A well-planned program and progressive sequence of physical education activities can provide for release of aggression in a socially acceptable manner.

5. EMOTIONAL REACTIONS DISPLAYED IN EARLY CHILDHOOD ARE LIKELY TO CONTINUE IN SOME FORM IN LATER YEARS. This could be one of the best reasons for providing physical education experiences for children. Through physical education experiences in the formative years we can help children develop constructive emotional reactions through a medium that they understand best —movement. Through the spontaneous freedom of expression of emotional reactions in the physical education experience, the real feelings of the child are more easily identified.

6. EMOTIONAL REACTIONS TEND TO INCREASE BEYOND NORMAL EXPECTANCY TOWARD THE CONSTRUCTIVE OR DESTRUCTIVE ON THE BALANCE OF FURTHERING OR HINDERING EXPERIENCES OF THE CHILD. For some children, the confidence they need to be able to face the problems of life may come about through physical expression. Therefore, physical education has tremendous potential to help contribute toward a solid base of total development.

7. DEPENDING ON CERTAIN FACTORS, A CHILD'S OWN FEELINGS MAY BE ACCEPTED OR REJECTED BY THE INDIVIDUAL. Children's physical education experiences should make them feel good and have confidence in themselves. Satisfactory self-concept is closely

related to body control; therefore, physical education experiences might be considered as one of the best ways of contributing to it.

OPPORTUNITIES FOR EMOTIONAL DEVELOPMENT THROUGH PHYSICAL EDUCATION

Physical educators have tended to give generous praise to their field for its potential to provide for emotional stability. The extent to which this actually accrues is dependent primarily upon the kind of emotional climate provided by the teacher and the physical education experiences provided for the children. For this reason it appears pertinent to examine some of the opportunities that exist for emotional development through physical education. The following descriptive list is submitted for this purpose.

1. RELEASE OF AGGRESSION IN A SOCIALLY ACCEPTABLE MANNER. This appears to be an outstanding way in which physical education experiences can help to make children more secure and emotionally stable. For example, kicking a ball in a game of kickball, batting a softball, or engaging in a combative stunt can afford a socially acceptable way of releasing aggression.

2. INHIBITION OF DIRECT RESPONSE OF UNPLEASANT EMOTIONS. This statement does not necessarily mean that feelings concerned with such unpleasant emotions as fear and anger should be completely restrained. On the contrary, the interpretation should be that such feelings can take place less frequently in a good physical education situation. This means that opportunities can be provided to relieve tension rather than to aggravate it.

3. PROMOTION OF PLEASANT EMOTIONS. Perhaps there is too much concern with suppressing unpleasant emotions and not enough attention given to the promotion of pleasant ones. One of the glorious things about physical education is that the range of activities is so great that there is "something for everybody." Thus, all children regardless of ability should be afforded the opportunity for success, at least most of the time.

4. FREEDOM FROM FEAR. This depends largely upon the approach taken by the teacher. As mentioned previously, when discussing a gymnastic activity, if the teacher says, "If you do it that way you will break your neck," such a negative approach can instill a fear that may not have existed originally.

5. RECOGNITION OF ONE'S ABILITIES AND LIMITATIONS. It has already been mentioned that the wide range of activities in physical education should provide an opportunity for success for all. This should make it easier to provide for individual differences of children so that all of them can progress within the limits of their own skill and ability.

6. UNDERSTANDING ABOUT THE ABILITY AND ACHIEVEMENTS OF OTHERS. In the physical education experience, emphasis can be placed upon achievement of the group along with the function of each individual in the group. Team play is the basis of many physical education activities.

7. BEING ABLE TO MAKE A MISTAKE WITHOUT BEING OSTRACIZED. This requires that the teacher serve as a catalyst who helps children understand the idea of trial and error. Emphasis can be placed on "trying" and that one can learn not only from his own mistakes, but from the mistakes of others as well.

The above discussion includes just a few examples of the numerous opportunities to help provide for emotional development through physical education. The resourceful and creative teacher will be able to expand this list manyfold. It bears repeating that emotional development through physical education will not accrue automatically. Although physical education theoretically provides a near-ideal setting for children to react in terms of ordinary behavior instead of highly emotional behavior, this situation does not always prevail. For instance, in cases where children are placed under stress in highly competitive situations over prolonged periods, there may be a strong possibility of detraction from, rather than a contribution to, their emotional stability.

In this particular connection, I recently asked the following question of about 200 fifth and sixth grade boys and girls: "What is the one thing that worries you most in school?" Although there was a wide variety of responses, the one general characteristic that tended to emerge was the emphasis placed on *competition* in so many school situations. Although the children did not state this specifically, the nature of their responses clearly seemed to be along these general lines.

Certainly there are many conditions in physical education that, if not carefully controlled, can cause *competitive stress*. This condition has been described by Scanlan and Passer as occurring when a child feels (perceives) that he or she will not be able to respond adequately to the performance demands of competition. When the child feels this way, he or she experiences considerable threat to self-esteem, which results in stress. They further describe competitive stress as the negative emotion or anxiety that a child experiences when he or she perceives the competition to be personally threatening.[1]

IMPLICATIONS OF RESEARCH
IN EMOTIONAL BEHAVIOR OF CHILDREN

It was mentioned in the preceding chapter that in a documentary analysis of research reported on elementary school physical education in the *Research Quarterly,* only 10 percent of these studies were concerned in some way with the emotional aspect of personality. Moreover, for the most part, these studies are not very definitive in terms of validity of the findings. This being the case, we can again turn to some of the psychological research that has been conducted in emotional development so that we might draw some implications for physical education. Reference is made again to the report of the National Institute of Education, which was mentioned in the preceding chapter. The following is a list of generalizations derived from the findings reported in the study of *aggression* in children and are accompanied by possible general implications for physical education. These implications are suggestive only, and the reader will no doubt be able to draw his or her own implications and make practical applications that apply to particular situations.

1. SUFFICIENT SPACE MAY ELIMINATE ACCIDENTAL PUSHING AND SHOVING THAT CAN LEAD TO RETALIATORY AGGRESSION. The implication for physical education should be obvious in that movement requires space in which to move. It may be recalled in Chapter Three, *space* was identified as a factor involved in movement and that there are two situations concerned with space. These are the amount of space required to perform a particular movement and the utilization of available space. It was further stated that

[1]T. K. Scanlan, and M. W. Passer, The psychological and social affects of competition, Los Angeles, 1977.

with regard to the latter it has been suggested that young children, during nonstructured self-initiated play, seem to reveal differences in the quantity of space they use and that these differences may be associated in important ways with other aspects of the child's development. Some studies tend to support the concept that space utilization of the young child in active play is a relatively stable dimension of his patterned behavior.

2. CHILDREN REWARDED FOR AGGRESSION LEARN THAT AGGRESSION PAYS OFF. This generalization is concerned with the extent to which a teacher uses praise for achievement. The teacher must be able to quickly discern whether success was due more to aggressive behavior than skill. The important thing here is the extent of aggressive behavior. Certainly a teacher should not thwart enthusiasm. It is sometimes difficult to determine whether an act was due to genuine enthusiasm or overt undesirable aggressive behavior.

3. CHILDREN INVOLVED IN CONSTRUCTIVE ACTIVITIES MAY BE LESS LIKELY TO BEHAVE AGGRESSIVELY. This implies that lessons should be well planned so that time is spent on constructive physical education activities. When this is accomplished it will be more likely that desirable and worthwhile learning will take place.

4. CHILDREN WHO HAVE ALTERNATIVE RESPONSES READILY AVAILABLE ARE LESS LIKELY TO RESORT TO AGGRESSION TO GET WHAT THEY WANT. This is concerned essentially with teacher-child relationships. While physical education generally involves group situations, there are many "one-on-one" opportunities between teacher and child. This gives the teacher a chance to verbalize to the child the kind of behavior that is expected under certain conditions. For example, a child who asks for an object such as a ball is more likely to receive cooperation. On the other hand, a child who grabs an object is more likely to elicit retaliatory aggression. Teacher reinforcement can increase children's use of nonaggressive solutions to interpersonal problems.

The teacher should be ready to intervene in a potentially aggressive situation before aggression occurs, encouraging children to use nonaggressive methods to solve conflicts. The teacher can provide verbal alternatives for those children who do not think of them for themselves. For example, "I am playing with this now," or "You can ask him to trade with you."

5. CHILDREN IMITATE BEHAVIOR OF PEOPLE THEY LIKE, AND THEY OFTEN ADOPT A TEACHER'S BEHAVIOR. Teachers of physical education are more likely to be a model adopted by children than would be the case with most other teachers. One of the reasons is that they meet the children on a much more informal basis. In addition, they deal with children in a curriculum area that is less inhibiting to children and one that is much more likely to be "fun oriented" than some of the other subject areas. Physical education teachers can take advantage of this situation by being nonaggressive in their own behaviors.

6. COOPERATION MAY BE INCOMPATIBLE WITH AGGRESSION. This could be interpreted to mean that the physical education teacher should consistently attend to and reinforce all cooperative behavior. Children consistently reinforced for cooperative behavior are likely to increase cooperative interactions while simultaneously decreasing aggressive behavior.

EVALUATING CONTRIBUTIONS OF PHYSICAL EDUCATION TO EMOTIONAL DEVELOPMENT

When we attempt to evaluate the emotional aspect of personality, we tend to encounter much the same situation as when we attempt to evaluate the social aspect. Included among some of the methods used for attempting to measure emotional responses are—

1. Blood pressure (it rises when one is under some sort of emotional stress).
2. Blood sugar analysis (under stressful conditions more sugar enters the bloodstream).
3. Pulse rate (emotional stress causes it to elevate).
4. Galvanic skin response (similar to the lie detector technique, and measurements are recorded in terms of perspiration in palms of hands).

These as well as others that have been used by investigators of human emotion have various and perhaps limited degrees of validity. In attempting to assess emotional reactivity, we oftentimes encounter the problem of the extent to which we are dealing with a purely physiological response or a purely emotional response. For example, one's pulse rate could be elevated by taking some sort of physical exercise. It could likewise be elevated if a person were the object of an embarrassing remark by another person. Thus, in this illustration the elevation of pulse rate could be caused for different reasons; the first being physiological and the second, emotional. Then, too, the type of emotional pattern is not identified by the measuring device; that is, a joy response and an anger response could show the same or nearly the same rise in pulse rate. These are some of the reasons why it is most difficult to arrive at a high degree of objectivity in studying the emotional aspect of personality.

A procedure that is designed to help teachers resolve some of the difficult problems of emotional adjustment is the *projective* technique. It has been suggested that this is a means by which a more or less neutral situation is given meaning by the individual responding to it; that is, by providing meaning or form to an "unstructured" setting, one "projects" his own feelings or perceptions into the stimulus situation.

Naturally, administration of any of the above procedures should be in the hands of specially prepared personnel for that purpose. In this regard, there may be a school psychologist available for consultation with teachers about emotional problems of children. Some schools routinely administer various kinds of personality scales. These can be perused by the teacher, but again it is likely that professional assistance will be needed for interpretation of information.

What we are essentially concerned with here is how an individual teacher can make some sort of valid evaluation of the extent to which physical education contributes to emotional development. This means that the teacher should make some attempt to assess physical education experiences with reference to whether or not these experiences are providing for emotional maturity.

One such approach would be to refer back to the list of "opportunities for emotional development through physical education" suggested previously in this chapter. These opportunities have been converted into a rating scale as follows:

1. The physical education experiences provide for release of aggression in a socially acceptable manner.
   4–most of the time
   3–some of the time
   2–occasionally
   1–infrequently

2. The physical education experiences provide for inhibition of direct response of unpleasant emotions.
   4–most of the time
   3–some of the time
   2–occasionally
   1–infrequently

3. The physical education experiences provide for promotion of pleasant emotion.
   4–most of the time
   3–some of the time
   2–occasionally
   1–infrequently

4. The physical education experiences provide for freedom from fear.
   4–most of the time
   3–some of the time
   2–occasionally
   1–infrequently

5. The physical education experiences provide for recognition of one's abilities and limitations.
   4–most of the time
   3–some of the time
   2–occasionally
   1–infrequently

6. The physical education experiences provide for an understanding about the ability and achievement of others.
   4–most of the time
   3–some of the time
   2–occasionally
   1–infrequently

7. The physical education experiences provide for being able to make a mistake without being ostracized.

4–most of the time
3–some of the time
2–occasionally
1–infrequently

If the teacher makes these ratings objectively and conscientiously, a reasonably good procedure for evaluation is provided. Ratings can be made periodically to see if positive changes appear to be taking place. Ratings can be made for a single experience, a group of experiences, or for the entire physical education program. This procedure can help the teacher identify the extent to which physical education experiences and/or conditions under which the experiences take place are contributing to emotional development.

Chapter Ten

INTELLECTUAL DEVELOPMENT OF CHILDREN THROUGH PHYSICAL EDUCATION

O F THE CONTRIBUTIONS that physical education makes to the total education of the child, the one concerned with intellectual development has been subjected to a great deal of criticism by some general educators. Close scrutiny of the possibilities of intellectual development through physical education reveals, however, that a very desirable contribution can be made through this medium. This belief is substantiated in part by the affirmations made by such eminent philosophers and educators as Plato, Locke, Rousseau, Pestalozzi, and numerous others. Plato's postulation that learning could take place better through play, Locke's thoughts on a sound mind and sound body, Rousseau's belief that all children should receive plenty of wholesome physical activity early in life, and Pestalozzi's observations that children approach their studies with a greater amount of interest after engaging in enjoyable physical activity have all contributed to the modern idea that physical education and intellectual development can have a high degree of compatibility.

With regard to the last-mentioned person, Johann Heinrich Pestalozzi (1746-1827), it has been suggested that this famous Swiss educator perhaps laid the foundation for modern teaching. He is considered one of the great pioneers concerned with the importance of child study as a basis for helping children learn. It has been reported that while observing his own child, Pestalozzi noticed that after playing for a time the boy tended to concentrate on his studies for an unusually long period. It is a matter of historical fact that many of the early elementary schools in this country were patterned after the philosophy of Pestalozzi. In view of this information, one could be tempted to rationalize that when physical education was first introduced into the elementary schools of the United States, its primary purpose was in the direction of contributing to intellectual pursuits of children. With the modern emphasis upon the possibilities of academic achievement through various forms of motor activity, I am tempted to speculate that we might have come full circle; that is, physical education for children may again be thought of mainly in terms of its potential contribution to intellectual development. I would certainly hesitate to impose this notion on others; nevertheless it is an interesting thought to ponder.

INTELLECTUAL NEEDS OF CHILDREN

In Chapter Three, on a discussion of intellectual fitness, the point was made that children have certain general intellectual needs: (1) a need for challenging experiences at the child's level of ability; (2) a need for intellectually successful and satisfying experiences; (3) a need for the opportunity to solve problems; and (4) a need for the opportunity to participate in creative experiences instead of always having to conform.

As in the case of physical, social, and emotional needs, children have certain specific intellectual needs. These specific needs can be reflected in the developmental characteristics of children. A number of intellectual characteristics are identified in the following lists at the different age levels.

Five-Year-Old Children

1. Enjoys copying designs, letters, and numbers.
2. Interested in completing tasks.
3. May tend to monopolize table conversation.
4. Memory for past events good.
5. Looks at books and pretends to read.
6. Likes recordings, words, and music that tell a story.
7. Enjoys counting objects.
8. Over 2,000 words in speaking vocabulary.

9. Can speak in complete sentences.
10. Can sing simple melodies, beat good rhythms, and recognize simple tunes.
11. Daydreams seem to center around make-believe play.
12. Attention span increasing up to twenty minutes in some cases.
13. Is able to plan activities.
14. Enjoys stories, dramatic plays, and poems.
15. Enjoys making up dances to music.
16. Pronunciation is usually clear.
17. Can express his needs well in words.

Six-Year-Old Children

1. Speaking vocabulary of over 2,500 words.
2. Interest span inclined to be short.
3. Knows number combinations up to ten.
4. Knows comparative values of the common coins.
5. Can define objects in terms of what they are used for.
6. Knows right and left side of body.
7. Has an association with creative activity and motorized life experience.
8. Drawings are crude but realistic and suggestive of early man.
9. Will contribute to guided group planning.
10. Conversation usually concerns his own experience and interests.
11. Curiosity is active and memory is strong.
12. Identifies himself with imaginary characters.

Seven-Year-Old Children

1. Abstract thinking is barely beginning.
2. Is able to listen longer.
3. Reads some books by himself.
4. Is able to reason, but has little experience upon which to base judgments.
5. The attention span is still short and retention poor, but does not object to repetition.

6. Reaction time is still slow.
7. Learning to evaluate the achievements of self and others.
8. Concerned with own lack of skill and achievement.
9. Becoming more realistic and less imaginative.

Eight-Year-Old Children

1. Can tell day of month and year.
2. Voluntary attention span increasing.
3. Interested in far-off places, and ways of communication now have real meaning.
4. Becoming more aware of adult world and his place in it.
5. Ready to tackle almost anything.
6. Shows a capacity for self-evaluation.
7. Likes to memorize.
8. Not always too good at telling time, but very much aware of it.

Nine-Year-Old Children

1. Individual differences are clear and distinct.
2. Some real interests are beginning to develop.
3. Beginning to have a strong sense of right and wrong.
4. Understands explanations.
5. Interests are closer to ten- or eleven-year-olds than to seven- or eight-year-olds.
6. As soon as a project fails to hold interest, it may be dropped without further thought.
7. Attention span is greatly increased.
8. Seems to be guided best by a reason, simple, and clear-cut, for a decision that needs to be made.
9. Ready to learn from occasional failure of his judgment as long as learning takes place in situations where failure will not have too serious consequences.
10. Able to make up own mind and come to decisions.
11. Marked reading disabilities begin to be more evident and may tend to influence the personality.
12. Range of interest in reading in that many are great readers while others may be barely interested in books.
13. Will average between six and seven words per remark.

Ten-Year-Old Children

1. Works with executive speed and likes the challenge of arithmetic.
2. Shows a capacity to budget his time and energy.
3. Can attend to a visual task and at the same time maintain conversation.
4. Some become discouraged and may give up trying when unsuccessful.
5. The attention span has lengthened considerably, with the child able to listen to and follow directions and retain knowledge more easily.
6. Beginning understanding of real causal relations.
7. Making finer conceptual distinctions and thinking reflectively.
8. Developing a scientific approach.
9. Better oriented with respect to time.
10. Ready to plan his day and accept responsibility for getting things done on time.

Eleven-Year-Old Children

1. Increasing power of attention and abstract reasoning.
2. Able to maintain a longer period of intellectual activity between firsthand experiences.
3. Interested in scientific experiments and procedures.
4. Can carry on many individual intellectual responsibilities.
5. Able to discuss problems and to see different sides of questions.
6. May lack maturity of judgment.
7. Increased language facility.
8. Attention span is increasing, and concentration may be given to a task for a long period of time.
9. Level of aspiration has increased.
10. Growing in ability to use several facts to make a decision.
11. Insight into causal relationships is developing more and is manifested by many how and why questions.

Twelve-Year-Old Children

1. Learns more ways of studying and controlling the physical world.
2. The use of language (on many occasions his own vocabulary) to exchange ideas for explanatory reasons.
3. More use of reflective thinking and greater ease of distinction.
4. Continuation in development of scientific approach.

It should be obvious that the above intellectual characteristics of children of different ages should be taken into account if we are to meet with any degree of success in our efforts in the direction of intellectual development through physical education.

GUIDELINES FOR INTELLECTUAL DEVELOPMENT

Guidelines for intellectual development are set forth here in the same manner that guidelines for physical, social, and emotional development through physical education were proposed in previous chapters; that is, these guidelines take the form of valid "concepts of intellectual development." When we have some sort of basis for the intellectual behavior of children as they grow and develop, we are then in a better position to provide physical education experiences that are likely to be compatible with intellectual development. The following list of concepts of intellectual development with implications for physical education are submitted with this general idea in mind.

1. CHILDREN DIFFER IN INTELLIGENCE. Teachers should be aware that poor performance of some children in physical education activities might be due to the fact that they have difficulty with communication. Differences in intelligence levels as well as in physical skill and ability need to be taken into account in the planning of physical education lessons.

2. MENTAL DEVELOPMENT IS RAPID IN EARLY CHILDHOOD AND SLOWS DOWN LATER. Children want and need challenging kinds of physical education experiences. Physical education lessons should be planned and taught in much the same way as other subjects of the elementary school curriculum. This precludes a pro-

gram that is devoted entirely to what has been called "nondirected play."

3. INTELLIGENCE DEVELOPS THROUGH THE INTERACTION OF THE CHILD AND HIS ENVIRONMENT. Movement experiences in physical education involve a process of interaction with the environment. There are many problem-solving opportunities in the well-planned physical education environment, and thus the child can be presented with challenging learning situations.

4. EMOTIONAL STRESS MAY AFFECT MEASURES OF INTELLIGENCE. Physical education experiences have potential value in the relief of emotional stress. This can possibly make the child more effective from an intellectual point of view.

5. EXTREMES IN INTELLIGENCE SHOW DIFFERENCES IN PERSONAL-ITY CHARACTERISTICS. The physical education teacher should be aware of the range of intelligence of children in a particular group. Experiences should be provided that challenge the so-called gifted child as well as meeting the needs of those children who are below average. In the physical education experience, children can learn to respect individual differences as far as levels of intelligence are concerned.

6. THE CHILD'S SELF-CONCEPT OF HIS ABILITY TO DEAL WITH INTELLECTUAL TASKS INFLUENCES HIS SUCCESSFUL DEALING WITH SUCH TASKS. The physical education experiences must contain a large degree of variation. This way it will likely insure that all children will achieve success at one time or another.

7. SITUATIONS THAT ENCOURAGE TOTAL PERSONALITY DEVELOP-MENT APPEAR TO PROVIDE THE SITUATIONS FOR INTELLECTUAL DE-VELOPMENT. The potential for total personality development is likely to be much more evident in physical education than in any other single subject area of the elementary school curriculum. If one were to analyze each of the subject areas for its potentialities for physical, social, emotional, and intellectual development, it is doubtful that any one of these areas would compare with the potential that is inherent in the physical education learning situation.

OPPORTUNITIES FOR INTELLECTUAL DEVELOPMENT THROUGH PHYSICAL EDUCATION

In Chapter 4 I arbitrarily classified three branches of physical education for children as: (1) curricular physical education, (2) compensatory physical education, and (3) cognitive physical education. Although there is much overlapping as far as these branches of physical education are concerned, they all have certain distinct features. For this reason, it appears logical to designate more or less specific opportunities for intellectual development in each of the three branches.

Opportunities for Intellectual Development Through Curricular Physical Education

It has been stated previously that of the contributions physical education makes to the total development of the child, the one concerned with intellectual development has been subjected to a great deal of criticism by some general educators. It has been demonstrated, however, that there are many potential opportunities for intellectual development through the medium of curricular physical education.

It is the general opinion of most learning theorists that problem solving is the major way of human learning; that is, learning tends to take place best when problem-solving opportunities are provided. In a well-taught physical education lesson there are numerous opportunities for children to exercise judgment and resort to reflective thinking in the solution of various kinds of problems. In fact, there are probably more opportunities for problem solving in the physical education experience than in most of the other subject areas. In addition, in a well-balanced physical education curriculum, children must acquire a knowledge of rules and regulations for various games. It is also important for effective participation that children gain an understanding of the various fundamentals and strategies involved in the performance of physical education activities.

Another very important aspect of intellectual development in curricular physical education is that which is concerned with the extent to which children can improve upon their listening skills.

In this particular connection, it has been observed that in the auditory-input phase of a physical education lesson, children "attend to" better than they do in this phase of a lesson in other subject areas. This means that in a well-taught physical education lesson, the child's attention is likely to be focused on the learning task and learning behavior.

It seems worth repeating that physical education need not be considered an "all brawn and no brain" segment of the elementary school curriculum when it is realized that the various factors mentioned above can contribute substantially to the intellectual development of children.

Opportunities for Intellectual Development Through Compensatory Physical Education

It should be recalled that my concept of compensatory physical education is that it attempts to correct various types of child learning disabilities that may stem from an impairment of the central nervous system and/or have their roots in certain social or emotional problems of children. This branch of physical education, most often through the medium of perceptual-motor development, involves the correction or at least some degree of improvement of certain motor deficiencies, especially those associated with fine-motor coordination.

Compensatory physical education, then, has the function of a more or less therapeutic means of improving upon certain perceptual-motor developmental features such as body concept, laterality and directionality, kinesthetic and tactile perception, and visual and auditory perception. In most physical education activities, one or more of these features are inherent aspects of the activity. Therefore, it appears logical to assume that experience gained in certain physical education activities can help to improve upon these features, which in turn might improve upon the child's ability to learn. Let us examine some of these possibilities in the broad categories of games, rhythmic activities, and gymnastic activities.

Games

The value of games as an important intellectual influence in the school program has been recognized for many decades. For example, as far back as 1909, Bancroft observed that a child's perceptions are quickened, he sees more quickly that the ball is coming toward him, that he is in danger of being tagged, or that it is his turn; he hears footsteps behind him, or his name or number called; he feels the touch on the shoulder; or in innumerable other ways he is aroused to quick and direct recognition of, and response to, things that go on around him.[1]

Rhythmic Activities

The various forms of rhythmic experiences have been used with some degree of success with children who have certain learning disabilities. Painter found that a program of systematic rhythmic and sensorimotor activities resulted in significant gains in body image, perceptual-motor integration, and psycholinguistic competence in low-functioning kindergarten children.[2]

In reporting about neurological dysfunctioning in the visual-perceptual-auditory motor areas, McClurg implied that disabled readers frequently lack coordination in such basic motor movements as walking and running and, further, that motor rhythm is often lacking in persons with reading, writing, and spelling problems.[3]

A very important rhythmic activity for children with learning disabilities is creative rhythms, where the child responds by expressing himself in a way that the rhythmical accompaniment makes him feel. When a child is able to use his body freely, there is a strong likelihood there will be increased body awareness. Creative rhythms will also give the child free self-direction in space, as well as self-control, in that he is not involved with a partner in a more formalized rhythmic activity. It has been found that creative rhythms provide a situation for children with learning disabilities where they cannot fail. There are no rules to remember and no criteria for good or bad; the only things he is asked to do is create his own ideas.

---

[1] J. H. Bancroft, *Games*, New York, Macmillan, 1909.
[2] G. Painter. The effect of a rhythmic and sensory-motor activity program on perceptual-motor spatial ability of kindergarten children, *Exceptional Children*, 33, 1969, p. 113.
[3] W. H. McClurg, The neurophysiological basis of reading disabilities, *The Reading Teacher*, April 1969.

Although great emphasis has been placed upon creative rhythms for the child with a learning disability, this should in no way minimize the value and importance of performing activities such as dancing, which are within the framework of an established pattern. For example, many forms of structured dance patterns contain various inherent perceptual-motor developmental factors as follows:

1. For children who have difficulty with sequencing (following a sequence of activities), dancing affords an opportunity to follow simple steps or procedures, which can lead to more complex patterns.
2. Dancing involves left and right directionality and at times may involve constant changing of directions.
3. The identification and use of certain parts of the body, such as arms, hands, feet, and legs are essential in some dances. Being called upon to use parts of the body may help establish one's image of body and body parts.
4. In activities such as singing games where accompaniment is furnished through song, it is the auditory clues that guide movement. Thus, an opportunity is provided for practice in auditory discrimination.

Gymnastic Activities

Certain stunt and tumbling activities can be of value in providing for perceptual-motor development. For example, since reading is a perceptual skill involving bilateral movement, certain stunts involving these movements may be used to advantage. It has also been found that certain stunts are useful in helping to improve body awareness. Stunts that alert the child to the movement of certain muscle groups when he presses against something can be of value for this purpose. One stunt is the *Back-to-Back Get Up*. This activity involves two children. They sit with their backs to each other and with their feet close to their buttocks. They lock arms at their elbows and keep them bent close to their sides. The two children then lean back against each other and straighten their legs until they are both in a standing position. They may need to use short walking steps to get to the standing position.

In tumbling activities involving some of the simple rolls, there is an opportunity to use those parts of the body, for example, the torso; less sensitive to *tactile* perception than other parts of the body. In this regard it has been suggested by Smith that through such tumbling activities as the *Log Roll,* the child is given the opportunity to explore the environment "tactilely" with the body and its segments.[4] The Log Roll is performed by having the child assume an extended prone position with his stomach facing the mat. The extended body position along the vertical axis is accomplished by placing the arms over the head along the mat until they are straight. The legs are also extended with the feet together and the toes pointed. The child then uses his head, shoulders, and hips to turn 360 degrees along the mat. The child should learn to roll in both directions and in a straight line down the mat.

Activities on the low balance beam can help the child maintain his relationship to gravity and at the same time help to develop space awareness and directionality-related movements.

Attempts to study the relationship between reading and ability to perform dynamic balance have yielded varying results. In one such study, Walker[5] compared balance beam walking test scores with reading readiness test scores of 162 first-grade children. On the basis of his data, he generalized that (1) there seemed to be a tendency for first-grade children, scoring high or low on the reading readiness test, to score respectively high or low on the balance beam walking test, (2) there seemed to be a much greater relationship between balance beam walking test scores and reading readiness test scores for girls than boys, and (3) girls tended to score higher than boys on the balance beam walking test. It is important to recognize that these are not cause-and-effect relationships, but coexistent behaviors.

---

[4]H. M. Smith, Implications for movement education experiences drawn from perceptual-motor research, *Journal of Health, Physical Education and Recreation,* April 1970.

[5]J. A. Walker, A comparison of Lee-Clark reading readiness scores with a test of balance using selected first grade children, Master's Thesis, U. of Maryland, College Park, 1963.

Opportunities for Intellectual Development
Through Cognitive Physical Education

I have been studying the phenomenon of cognitive physical education for the better part of three decades. During this time, I have published five textbooks and over fifty research reports and position papers on the subject. Most of this work has referred to the phenomenon as "child learning through motor activity." As a consequence, in recent years a number of learning theorists have identified it as the "Humphrey Program of Child Learning Through Motor Activity." However, for purposes of this book, I will stay with the term *cognitive physical education,* having identified it as one of the branches of physical education for children.

In Chapter Four cognitive physical education was discussed in relation to theory, inherent facilitative learning factors, and its future prospects. In addition, a couple of examples of cognitive physical education learning activities were presented. In the present discussion of opportunities for intellectual development through cognitive physical education, I will present a few additional examples representative of these learning activities. The examples include an application and evaluation of the learning activity. (Over the years, I have developed over two thousand of these kinds of learning activities in the curriculum areas of reading and language arts, mathematics, science, social studies, and health and safety. Examples given here will be confined to reading, mathematics, and science.)

Reading

Concept: The understanding that each sound has a definite form and that each form has a definite sound (auditory-visual perception).

Activity: Stop, Look, and Listen. The children stand in a line—one beside the other. The teacher holds up a letter of the alphabet. At the same time, the teacher calls out a word that *does* or *does not* begin with that sound. If the word does not begin with that sound, the children do not run. If the word begins with that sound, the children run toward a prearranged goal line to see who can get there first.

Application: Auditory-visual perception is an important part of the readiness and word analysis program in first grade. This game can be used as children get the first sight words in order to secure auditory-visual perception.

Evaluation: This game was a good test of how well the children learned the sound of the element and how well they knew the form of the element. Children liked being able to tell whether the sound was the same as the one spoken, and they liked the aspect of suspense as to when the word would be called on which they could run.

Concept: Distinguishing long vowel sounds with the same consonant blend beginning.

Activity: Crows and Cranes. The class is divided into two equal groups, the Crows and the Cranes, who stand facing each other on two parallel lines three to five feet apart. A goal line is drawn twenty to thirty feet behind each group. The teacher or leader calls out the name of one of the groups—Crows or Cranes. Members of the group whose name is called run and try to reach their goal line before they are tagged by any member of the other group. All of those tagged become members of the opposite group. The groups then return to their original places, and the same procedure is followed. The group having the greatest number of players on its side at the end of the playing period wins the game.

Application: The children and the classroom teacher had discussed sounds of consonants and several consonant blends in reading class. Later, vowels were discussed, beginning with long sounds. In making lists of words having long vowel sounds, the children discovered that the bird names "crows" and "cranes" require careful listening to determine which vowel was to be pronounced. Children running in the wrong direction had to leave their own group and become members of the other group.

Evaluation: The children soon learned that each must remember which bird he was supposed to be. He would not know when to run until he heard the name of the bird and compared the sound with his own bird name. It was discovered that words may have the same beginning sound, but vowel sounds make different words and make them have different meanings, as in "crows" and "cranes."

Mathematics

Concept: We divide to find the number of sets.

Activity: Get Together. Players take places around the activity area in a scattered formation. The leader calls any number by which the total number of players is not exactly divisible. The players try to form groups of the number called. Each group joins hands in a circle. The one or ones left out have points scored against them. Low score wins the game.

Application: This activity may be useful at about the third-grade level. Numbers called usually should be 2, 3, 4, 5, or 10, since these are numbers with which they learn to divide at this level.

Evaluation: This activity was good for reinforcing the idea of sets and that they are like things (in this case children). It also gave the children the idea that there might be a *remainder* when dividing into groups.

Concept: The number above the line in a fraction is the numerator, which tells the number of parts of the whole; the number below the line in a fraction is the denominator, which tells how many parts make up the whole.

Activity: Couple Tag. Players are scattered around the activity area in groups of two. One player is "it." "It" tries to grasp the free hand of one member of a couple, and, if he succeeds, the other member becomes "it" and the game continues.

Application: The teacher developed with the class the idea that, in this game, a group of two equaled one whole. The number of children in the class was ascertained to be the numerator of the fraction, since it told the number of "parts" with which they were dealing. The number of children in each group (in this case, two) was ascertained to be the denominator of the fraction, since it told how many parts made up the whole. The class recognized the fact that this was an improper fraction and that it would be necessary to divide the denominator into the numerator in order to find how many "wholes" or whole teams there would be and what fractional part of a team would be left over. In successive experiences with this activity, the game was called *Triplet Tag, Quartet Tag,* and *Sextet Tag,* as the denominator of the fraction was increased.

Evaluation: This game was effective in helping the children relate the fractional concept and the terms "numerator" and "denominator" to real-life situations. As the numerator of the fraction changed with the number of children needed to make up each "whole" or tag group, the terms of various fractions became more real and useful to them. They realized that they actually use fractions in their activities without being conscious of it.

Science

Concept: Shadows are formed by the sun shining on various objects.

Activity: Shadow Tag. The players are dispersed over the playing area, with one person designated as "it." If "it" can step on or get into the shadow of another player, that player becomes "it." A player can keep from being tagged by getting into the shade or by moving in such a way that "it" finds it difficult to step on his shadow.

Application: During the science period the classroom teacher gave the definition of a shadow. A discussion led the class to see how shadows are made as well as why they move. The class then went outside the room where many kinds of shadows were observed. Since each child had a shadow, it was decided to put them to use in playing the game.

Evaluation: The children saw how the sun causes shadows. By playing the game at different times during the day they also observed that the length of the shadow varied with the time of day. The activity proved very successful for illustrating shadows.

Concept: Things that are balanced have equal weights on either side of their central point.

Activity: Rush and Tug. This is a combative activity, and the class is divided into two groups with each group standing behind one of two parallel lines about forty feet apart. In the middle of these two parallel lines, a rope is laid perpendicular to them. A cloth is tied to the middle of the rope to designate both halves of the rope. On a signal, members of both groups rush to their half of the rope, pick it up and tug toward the group's end line. The group pulling the midpoint of the rope past its own end line in a specified amount of time is declared the winner. If at the end of the designated time, the midpoint of the rope has not been pulled beyond one group's line, the group with the midpoint of the rope nearer to its end line is declared the winner.

Application: In performing this combative activity, it was decided to have the group experiment with all kinds of combinations of teams, such as boys versus boys, birls versus girls, boys versus girls, big ones against little ones, and mixed sizes and weights against the same.

Evaluation: This was a very stimulating experience for the group, since it presented to them a genuine problem-solving situation in trying to get the exact combination of children for an equal balance of the two teams. When there was enough experimenting, two teams of equal proportions were assembled, and it was found that it was most difficult for either to make any headway. They also discovered that an equal balance depended not only on the weight of their classmates, but to a great extent upon their strength. Other classes, where the physical education learning medium had not been used, showed much less interest in this important concept. It was speculated that this was perhaps due to the fact that the procedure presented problem-solving situations that were of immediate interest and concern to the children in a concrete manner.

RESEARCH WHICH SUPPORTS CONTRIBUTIONS OF PHYSICAL EDUCATION TO INTELLECTUAL DEVELOPMENT

In previous chapters it was suggested that research has not been too definitive with regard to the contribution that physical education gives to the physical, social, and emotional development of children. The same may be said generally of intellectual development. Nevertheless, attempts have been made to place an objective foundation under the long-held theoretical postulation that physical education can contribute to the intellectual pursuits of children. My own efforts in this direction have met with a relative degree of success according to attestations of some prominent learning theorists.

The research reported here is concerned with studies that I have either conducted or directed. (The reader should understand that I am well aware that other studies have been undertaken to assess the potential contribution of physical education to intellectual development of children. I have arbitrarily chosen to use my own approach as one means of studying this phenomenon.)

Research Techniques

There are a number of acceptable ways of studying how behavioral changes take place in children. After some amount of study and experimentation, a certain sequence of techniques emerged as the most appropriate way to evaluate how well children might learn through the physical education medium. These techniques can generally be classified as: (1) naturalistic observation, (2) single-group experimental procedure, (3) parallel group experimental procedure, and (4) variations of standard experimental procedures.

Naturalistic Observation

One of the first problems to be reckoned with was whether this type of learning activity could be accomplished in the regular school situation, and also whether teachers would subscribe to this particular approach. To obtain this information, a procedure that could best be described as *naturalistic observation* was used. This involved the teaching of a skill or concept in a particular subject area to a group of children and using a physical education activity in which the skill or concept was inherent. The teacher would then evaluate how well the skill or concept was learned through the physical education learning medium. The teacher's criteria for evaluation were his or her past experiences with other groups of children and other learning media. The immediately preceding section of this chapter gives some representative cases of the process of naturalistic observation.

This procedure is grossly lacking in objectivity because there is only a subjective evaluation of the teacher to support the hypothesis. However, in the early stages of the work this technique served the purpose well, because at that time the main concern was having teachers experiment with the idea and to ascertain their reaction to it. In a vast majority of cases the reactions of teachers were very positive. Incidentally, over two thousand naturalistic observations were made over about a six-year period.

Single Groups

The next factor that needed to be taken into consideration was whether or not children could actually learn through the physical education learning medium. Although, for centuries empirical evidence had placed the hypothesis in a very positive position, there was still the need for some objective evidence to support the hypothesis. In order to determine if learning could actually take place through the physical education medium, the *single group technique* was employed. This technique involved the criterion measure of objective pretesting of a group of children on certain skills or concepts in a given subject area. Physical education activities in which the skills or concepts were involved, were taught to the children over a specified period of time and used as learning activities to develop the skills or concepts. After the specified period of time, the children were retested and served as their own controls for comparing results of the posttest with the results of the pretest.

All of the studies involving this technique in which the subjects were their own controls showed significant differences between pretest and posttest scores at a very high level of probability. Therefore, it appeared reasonable to generalize that learning actually could take place through the physical education learning medium.

Parallel Groups

With the preceding information at hand, the next step and obviously the most important one in the sequence of research techniques was to attempt to determine how the physical education learning medium compared with other more traditional media.

For this purpose, the *parallel group technique was used.* This technique involved pretesting children on a number of skills or concepts in a given subject area and equating them into groups. One group was designated as the physical education group (experimental group) , and an attempt was made to develop the skills or concepts through the physical education learning medium. The other group was designated as the traditional group (control group) , and an attempt was made to develop the skills or concepts through one or more traditional media. Both groups were taught by the same teacher over a specified period of time. At the end of the experiment, both groups were retested, and comparisons were made of the posttest scores of both groups.

Variations of Standard Experimental Procedures

Along with the above, a number of variations of standard techniques were employed. In studying the effectiveness of the physical education learning medium for boys compared to girls, a procedure was used that involved parallel groups of boys and girls within the total single group.

In those cases where an attempt was made to hold a certain specific variable constant, three groups were used. In this situation, one group became an observing or nonparticipating group.

Another variation was to equate children into two groups with each group taught by a different teacher. This was done for the purpose of comparing a physical education teacher who would not likely be skilled in teaching concepts in another curriculum area with a superior classroom teacher who would likely be highly skilled in this direction.

In most of the studies, the experiment was carried on over a period of ten days. (In some cases where conditions permitted, this time period was longer.) There were ordinarily eight and sometimes as many as ten skills or concepts involved. A ten-day period allowed for two days of testing and eight days of teaching. Reliability for the objective tests was ordinarily obtained by using a test-retest with similar groups of children. All of the experiments were done in the actual school situation. Obviously, it would be better to carry them out over extended periods of time, but in most cases it was impractical to do so because it usually involved some interruption in the school program.

Some Representative Research Findings

Over a period of years, a relatively large number of controlled studies have been carried out utilizing the various techniques reported in the preceding section of the chapter. Following are some examples representative of these studies in the areas of reading, mathematics, and science.

In a study involving reading skills, twenty third-grade children were equated into two groups.[6] One group was taught through physical education activities in the form of active games. The other group was taught through traditional language workbooks. Both groups had the same teacher. Comparisons were made of the pretest and posttest scores of the language workbook group and also the active game group. The statistical analysis showed that both groups learned, but that the active game group learned at a higher level of significance. When the posttest scores of both groups were analyzed, it was indicated that the active game group learned significantly more than the language workbook group.

In recognition of the limitations imposed by a study of this nature, it was generalized that if one accepts the significant differences in the test scores as evidence of learning, these third-grade children developed language comprehension through both active games and the traditional language workbook medium, although the active game group produced greater changes.

Another study involving reading skills was designed to evaluate the effectiveness of active games as a means of reinforcing reading skills with fourth-grade children.[7] The purpose of this study was to determine how well certain reading skills could be reinforced by physical education activities in the form of active games as compared with some of the traditional ways of reinforcing these skills.

Seventy-three fourth-grade children were pretested on eight reading skills. Thirty of these children were divided into two groups. One group of fifteen was designated as the active game

---

[6] J. H. Humphrey, Comparison of the use of active games and language workbook exercise as learning media in the development of language understandings with third-grade children, *Perceptual and Motor Skills*, 21:23, 1965.

[7] J. H. Humphrey, The use of the active game learning medium in the reinforcement of reading skills with fourth-grade children. *The Journal of Special Education*, 1:369, 1967.

group and the other group of fifteen as the traditional group. Each reading skill was introduced and presented to the two groups together. The groups were then separated, and, with one group, the reading skills were reinforced through the form of active games. With the other group, the reading skills were reinforced by such traditional media as a language workbook, a dictionary, and prepared ditto sheets. Both groups were taught by the same teacher. The types of reading skills used in the study were structural analysis, phonics, word recognition, and vocabulary development.

After the reading skills were presented in the manner described, both groups were retested. The experiment covered ten school days, allowing one day for pretesting, eight days for the experiment, and a final day for posttesting. A comparison of the posttest mean scores showed that the active game group learned significantly more than the traditional group. Therefore, it was concluded that the kinds of reading skills used in this study could be reinforced to better advantage by active games than by some more traditional approaches.

A study in the area of mathematics is an example of a single group experimental procedure with parallel groups of boys and girls within the single group.[8] The purpose of this study was to determine how well a group of first-grade children develop number concepts through physical education activities and, at the same time, to ascertain whether the approach was more favorable for boys or for girls.

Thirty-five first-grade children were pretested on eight number concepts that were to be included as a part of their regular class work during the ensuing two weeks. Ten boys and ten girls who had the same pretest scores were selected for the experiment. Eight active games in which the number concepts were involved and deemed appropriate for use at first-grade level were selected.

The active games were taught to the twenty children and used as learning media for the development of the number concepts. They were retested after the active game medium was used. The statistical analysis showed that as a total single group there was a

[8]J. H. Humphrey, An exploratory study of active games in learning of number concepts by first-grade boys and girls, *Perceptual and Motor Skills,* 23, 1966.

highly significant difference from pretest to posttest mean scores. In comparing boys with girls, the results indicated greater changes in learning were produced with the boys.

Another study in the area of mathematics was conducted to explore statistically the relationships between the traditional and physical education activities the classroom teacher and physical education teacher used in teaching selected mathematical concepts to first-grade children.[9] A secondary purpose was to see if first-grade children could learn selected mathematical concepts through the physical education medium when taught by the physical education teacher.

The regular first-grade classroom teacher taught the number concept to the control group by traditional classroom techniques, and the experimental group was taught by the physical education teacher by use of physical education activities. The teaching time for the two groups involved nine class periods of thirty minutes each. At the conclusion of the nine class periods the two groups were retested to see if there were statistically significant differences in the two teaching techniques as taught by the classroom teacher and the physical education teacher.

In the experimental group, taught by the physical education teacher, a statistical analysis of the data indicated a difference at an extremely high level of probability from pretest to posttest. In the control group taught by the classroom teacher there was also a significant difference, but at a lower level of probability than for the experimental group. When the posttest scores of both groups were compared there was a significant difference in favor of the experimental group at a moderately high level of probability.

Any conclusions to be drawn from a study of this nature must be governed by a degree of caution. However, the following generalizations seemed warranted: (1) the experimental group indicated a trend toward a more uniform rate of learning as indicated by the standard deviations of both groups, (2) physical education activities could be used with success in helping slower

---

[9]E. A. Trout, A comparative study of selected mathematical concepts developed through physical education activities taught by the physical education teacher, and traditional techniques taught by the classroom teacher, Master's Thesis, U. of Maryland, College Park, 1969.

learning children learn about mathematics, and (3) the physical education teacher could serve as a consultant when formulating the first-grade mathematics curriculum.

In a study in the area of science, two groups of slower learning fifth-grade children were equated on the basis of pretest scores on science concepts.[10]   One group was designated as the physical education group and the other as the traditional group.   The IQ range of the physical education group was 74 to 89, with a mean of 85.   The traditional group's IQ range was 72 to 90, with a mean of 83.   The children were tested three times.   After the first test had been administered to a large group, two groups of ten were selected.   Both groups were taught the same science concepts by the same teacher, one through traditional procedures and the other through the physical education learning medium.   The teaching was over a two-week period at the time the children were retested.   Following this second test, there was no formal instruction on the science concepts that were taught during this two-week period.   They were tested a third time at an interval of three months after the second test.

The difference in means scores was used as the criterion for learning.   When analyzed statistically, it was found that the physical education group learned significantly more than the traditional group.   Also, the physical education group showed a higher level of retention for the three-month period.   Although the traditional group retained what was learned, the gain in learning was minimal to begin with.

Another study involved the reinforcement or enrichment of science concepts through physical education.[11]   Twenty-three first-grade children were pretested on a science unit on simple machines.   The children were equated into two groups.   The classroom teacher taught eight science lessons to the entire class of twenty-three children to illustrate eight first-grade science con-

---

[10]J. H. Humphrey, The use of motor activity in the development of science concepts with slow learning fifth grade children, *Journal of Research in Science Teaching,* 9, no. 3, 1972.

[11]I. H. Prager, The use of physical education activities in the reinforcement of selected first-grade science concepts, Master's Thesis, U. of Maryland, College Park, 1968.

cepts involving simple machines. The teacher used regular traditional teaching procedures with the class.

Immediately after each lesson the physical education teacher took eleven of the children (experimental group) on the basis of the pretest scores and attempted to reinforce the concepts through various kinds of physical education activities.

After the procedure was followed for a two-week period, all of the children were retested. The results of this posttest showed that the group whose learning was reinforced by the physical education teacher was significantly greater than the group not reinforced by such procedures. In comparing each group separately as its own control, it was indicated that the group reinforced by the physical education medium gained significantly at a very high level of probability while the other group did not improve significantly. The results also showed that the reinforcement procedure was more favorable for boys than for girls at this age level.

On the basis of the results of this study, the following generalizations appeared warranted: (1) the activities taught by the physical education teacher should be considered as a reinforcement aid in teaching first-grade science concepts; (2) this procedure should be given consideration in developing science concepts with first-grade boys because the results were so favorable to learning for boys; (3) the physical education teacher should be considered an important consultant in the planning of certain types of learning experiences in the science curriculum.

SOME GENERALIZATIONS OF THE RESEARCH FINDINGS

In view of the fact that there are now some objective data to at least partially support a long-held hypothetical postulation, perhaps some generalized assumptions along with some reasonable speculations can be set forth with some degree of confidence. Obviously, the available data are not extensive enough to carve out a clear-cut profile with regard to learning through the physical education medium. However, they are suggestive enough to give rise to some interesting generalizations, which may be briefly summarized as follows:

1. In general, children tend to learn certain academic concepts

better through the physical education learning medium than through many of the traditional media.

2. This approach, while favorable for both boys and girls, appears to be more favorable for boys.
3. The approach appears to be more favorable for children with average and below average intelligence.
4. For children with high levels of intelligence, it may be possible to introduce more advanced concepts at an earlier age through the physical education learning medium.

It will remain the responsibility of further research to provide more conclusive evidence to support these generalizations and speculations. There is hope, however, based on actual experience with this approach, to encourage those responsible for facilitating child learning of academic concepts to use this approach and to join in collecting evidence to verify the contribution of the physical education learning medium to the education curriculum.

EVALUATING CONTRIBUTIONS OF PHYSICAL EDUCATION TO INTELLECTUAL DEVELOPMENT

How does the physical education teacher estimate or place a value on whether or not children are developing intellectually as a result of their physical education experiences? One of the first factors to take into account is the extent to which the physical education teacher is aware of the inherent possibilities for intellectual development in the physical education experience. I say this kindly because there are some teachers who are not cognizant of the fact that such possibilities exist. This means that physical education teachers should analyze the content of the program and the manner in which it is conducted; that is, what are the opportunities for such experiences as auditory and visual perception, problem solving, along with a host of other intellectually oriented experiences? When the teacher recognizes the inherency of such possibilities, he or she is then in a better position to observe for intellectual growth through physical education.

One of the best procedures that I have found for evaluation of the contribution physical education is making to intellectual development is for the physical education teacher to maintain a close liaison with classroom teachers. In this way, he or she can become more aware of the extent to which experiences in physical education are coordinated with classroom experiences in the other subject areas. Let us say, for example, that the physcial education teacher is aware that Miss Jones, a third-grade teacher, is currently dealing with the subject of fractions in her classroom. If it is appropriate, the physical education teacher could start out his or her class by saying something like the following: "Miss Jones tells me that you are working fractions in her class. In our class today we will be doing some activities in which it could be important to know something about fractions." The teacher could then proceed to indicate the ways fractions are involved in the particular situation and to ask children to think of other ways. There could be a follow-up later with the classroom teacher to see if this experience carried over and correlated with the classroom experience. Such possibilities are almost unlimited, and the creative and resourceful physical education teacher will capitalize upon them.

In summarizing this chapter, I think it can be seen that there are infinite potentialities for intellectual development of children through physical education. John Dewey, one of the most notable educators of this century, may have expressed it best over sixty years ago with the statement; "Experience has shown that when children have a chance at *physical activities,* which bring their natural impulses into play, going to school is a joy, management is less of a burden, and *learning is easier.*"[12]

It seems appropriate to end the book with this classic statement; because John Dewey was perhaps the first proponent for the concept of "learning by doing." Physical education epitomizes the possibilities for learning by doing, because it is a major function of this discipline to help children learn to move and move to learn.

---

[12]J. Dewey, *Democracy and Education,* An Introduction to the Philosophy of Education, New York, Macmillan, 1919, p. 228-229.

INDEX

189

cation, 144-161
opportunities for, through physical
education, 154-156
intellectual, 162-187
evaluating contributions of physical
education to, 187-188
guidelines for, through physical
education, 167-168
of children, through physical education, 162-187
opportunities for, through physical
education, 169-178
research which supports contributions of physical education to,
178-186
meaning of, 24-25
physical, 107-123
evaluating contributions of physical
education to, 115-119
extent to which physical education
contributes to, 111-113
guidelines for, through physical
education, 113-115
of children through physical education, 107-123
social, 124-143
evaluating contributions of physical
education to, 141-143
guidelines for, through physical
education, 129-132
of children through physical education, 124-143
some possibilities of, through physical education, 132-135
total, 23-33
meaning of, 23
Dewey, John, 8, 80, 188
Directionality of sound, 99
Dodging, 69
Domains, 25-26
affective, 25
cognitive, 25
learning, 25
psychomotor, 26
Domian, O. E., 136

E

Emotional control, 37-38

Endurance, 116-117
circulatory-respiratory, 116-117
muscular, 116
Evaluation, 102-104, 141-143, 158-161,
187-188
of contributions of physical education
to emotional development, 158-161
of contributions of physical education
to intellectual development, 187-188
of contributions of physical education
to physical development, 115-119
Extraclass physical education, 41

F

Fabricius, H., 112
Falling, 79
Fatigue, 8
Fear, 146-147
Fitness, 115-119, 125-126
physical, 115-119
components of, 116-117
social, 125-126
Flexibility

G

Galloping, 66
Games, 76-79, 170-171
meaning of, 76
progression in, 77-79
Gardner, E. B., 60
Good, C. V., 23, 51
Gymnastic activities, 83-84, 172-173
meaning of, 83
value of, 84

H

Halverson, L. E., 73
Hanson, M. R., 58
Historical background of physical edu-
cation for children, 6-9
Holmes, M., 8
Hopping, 65-66
Horrocks, R. N., 134
Humphrey, J. H., 46, 56, 182, 183, 185

I

Interaction, 98-99
child-child, 98-99
teacher-child, 99